Best wishes on all
your biggest hunts!

Advance Praise for **Whale Hunting**

"WHALE HUNTING is the type of business book that I wish we saw more of. It has a specific and well-defined purpose—to teach managers how to land really big accounts—and it delivers on that purpose in a clear, practical, convincing, and entertaining way. I can tell you that it not only maps well into the big-account sales process but it also makes for fascinating reading. Simply put, it works."

—*Dave Godes, Associate Professor of Business Administration, Harvard University*

"Searcy and Smith introduce a nine-phase sales cycle to help small- to mid-sized companies accelerate their growth by capturing a 'whale.' *Whale Hunting* shows readers how to create this process and duplicate it again and again. A must-read for anyone who is trying to capture a whale of their own!"

—*Cathy Langham, President of Langham Logistics*

Whale | Hunting

Whale | Hunting

How to Land Big Sales and Transform
Your Company

Tom Searcy and Dr. Barbara Weaver Smith

John Wiley & Sons, Inc.

For general information on our other products and services or for technical support,
please contact our Customer Care Department within the United States at (800)
762-2974, outside the United States at (317) 572-3993 or fax (317) 572-4002.

Wiley also publishes its books in a variety of electronic formats. Some content that
appears in print may not be available in electronic books. For more information about
Wiley products, visit our web site at www.wiley.com.

ISBN-13 9780470182697

Printed in the United States of America

10 9 8

We dedicate this book to Jen Searcy and Larry Smith,
with love and gratitude.

Contents

Foreword

WHALE HUNTING is a confluence of business writing, practical skills, and consumerism. It should resonate with anyone who runs a business—if not, they won't be in business very long. Tom Searcy and Barbara Weaver Smith, through their unique partnership and history of successful entrepreneurship, serve up whale hunting as the DNA of service-focused organizations.

Whale Hunting has a mission and a message that are easy to understand. The book is interesting and fun. The authors' method resonates in a way that other sales approaches don't. Typical sales training doesn't change the vernacular, but whale hunting, through its metaphor and language, gets people excited about thinking differently.

As I read the principles and ideals of the whale hunting philosophy expressed in this book, it struck me that every company faces the problems that Searcy and Smith illustrate, and then resolve.

I live on the service side of the business world; everything we do is about expanding and improving on the service to our customers.

My company is quite large. We have 1,100 employees in the United States and 2,300 globally, and we are part of Omnicom Group, which employs more than 70,000 worldwide. In many regards, we'd easily be categorized as "the whale." So, how can we push ourselves to remain nimble, creative, active, and prosperous?

It's a real challenge. Big companies often develop a sense of confidence that little fish will get caught in our wake even if we are not working too hard. But no matter what your company's size, unless you are constantly on a whale hunt, you will atrophy. Even if you are as successful as we are, even if you are ranked number one in your market globally, your competitors are "predator modeling"—they are plotting new ways and approaches to take you down. Figuratively and metaphorically, they view you as a whale, believing the odds are that you have become bloated, cumbersome, and slow, whereas they are lean, agile, and quick.

How do you retain your number-one position, and maintain the energy and momentum that helped you to grow, while more nimble and hungrier villagers are trying to take food off your table? Help your team realize that they shouldn't be waiting for another giant RFP to come over the transom? That you must continually hunt in order to eat? Changing that mind-set is a very significant culture issue, and whale hunting is right on target.

If that's true for a global marketing firm, how much more true might it be for your business? Whale hunting is how you gain or recapture the spirit of the hunt. *Whale Hunting* promotes a disciplined, unrelenting pursuit of advantage and growth. In the book, you learn that everybody in the company is a salesperson, all working in collaboration with others. "Sales" is not a dirty word—no matter what your role, it's okay and, in fact, essential to ask people to buy from you. If you don't ask for the order and the sale, someone else will.

The Whale Hunters understand how the economy has changed, especially with technology and consumer-controlled marketing. Consumers are in control of what they see, when they see it, how they see it, and how they buy.

We used to practice interruption-based marketing. Today's customers hate being interrupted. The whales—those customers whose potential deal is 10 to 20 times the size of your average deal—will hate to be interrupted. As a marketer, a salesperson, a CEO, you need to learn how to run alongside of them and create new ways for them to experience your brand and your promise. You have to understand differently. *Whale Hunting* will help you gain that understanding.

I'm very bullish about *Whale Hunting* because the business principles are illustrative in ways that others are not. Many books about sales are esoteric and irrelevant, but *Whale Hunting* is rooted in basic business principles. Through a brilliant metaphor, *Whale Hunting* presents core principles of Business 101 in a new and engaging fashion. These principles include:

- Pay attention.
- Prepare.
- Go on the hunt.
- Assign everyone a role.
- Take the necessary time.
- Store up for the cold spells.
- Let no one take food off your table.

When I talk to people in business, I speak in analogous ways because, in my opinion, an analogy is very powerful and easily understood. I'm a Yankees fan, yet the 2007 team is composed of great individual contributors who are all waiting for the big pitch;

they are not getting on base, manufacturing runs, stealing bases, playing the numbers game that says on-base percentages correlate with wins. While they wait for the chance to do magic, their competitors take deliberate, disciplined approaches to run production. And the Yankees lose, despite their awesome talent.

My point is that, attitudinally, it all ties in with business. You can't wait for the big pitch. You need to manufacture every run. That's what *Whale Hunting* is about—systematically and repeatedly developing a sales process that's as replicable as advanced manufacturing. If you understand that need, this book will resonate for you as it resonates with business owners, leaders, marketers, and sales teams.

The only other author I know who has achieved this is Malcolm Gladwell, in *Blink*. *Whale Hunting* is Gladwell-esque, providing more fundamentals than theory. Searcy and Smith are smart people who think about business the way I do. Their method has helped dozens of small to midsize businesses achieve extraordinary growth in relatively short periods of time. And I can attest to its appeal for big companies as well.

Whoever you are, whatever your business, you are not too small or too big to improve your sales productivity through the lessons in *Whale Hunting*. Buy this book, read it, implement its lessons. You will make whale hunting a way of life.

James Lyons, President, North America
Rapp Collins Worldwide
Full-service, direct marketing agency with
50 offices in 30 countries

Preface

WHALE HUNTING. The name itself conjures up images of whales breaching in icy seas, harpoons slicing through the frosty nighttime air, and groups of people, clothed in massive furs, huddled along the shore waiting for the hunters' glorious return. How do such images relate to rapid business growth?

Directly and powerfully.

Ever since Tom visited an Inuit museum in the northwestern United States, we've been exploring the analogy between whale hunting and business growth. In the process, we've learned a great deal about the remarkable whale hunting processes of the Inuit people of northwest Alaska. At a turning point in their history—born perhaps of desperate need or of opportunities made possible by new tools, skills, and knowledge—the Inuit ceased to wait patiently for the occasional whale to beach itself during the spring migration. They ceased to be satisfied with a diet of fish or seals or the occasional caribou. Rather, they set out to hunt whales—deliberately, strategically, and mindfully, utilizing every resource that their village could offer. We believe they did so because while a smaller catch might feed one family for a week, a whale would feed the village for a year.

In our lexicon, *a whale is a very big deal, 10 to 20 times larger than your average deal, typically with a company that is bigger than yours.* *Whale Hunting* is about small to midsized companies accelerating—even exploding—their growth by learning to sell and to service whale-sized deals as a matter of routine rather than as an occasional exception.

Our continuing study of Inuit whale hunting methods, coupled with Tom's experience in rapid business development and Barbara's background in culture change, inspired a sales process model that we have implemented successfully within many small and midsize companies, some of whose experiences we share in the chapters to follow. We have also worked with independent sales professionals and the sales organizations of large companies.

The Inuit approached a whale in a small boat, manned by small crews, far from land and safety. If they could land a whale, their families and villages would thrive. But if they failed, the people might well starve during an upcoming bitter winter as a consequence of a single unsuccessful hunting season.

We have developed a process for whale hunting derived from and illustrated by those ancient ways and enhanced by our more contemporary experiences. In this book, we elaborate the methods Inuit used to scout, hunt, and harvest their whales. We identify and explain nine phases of the whale hunt, in each phase relating the Inuit practice to modern business. Our purpose is to explain how you can help your company repeatedly land and service those big deals that transform your business, no matter what your role in management, sales, operations, or customer service.

You know intuitively that successfully hunting a new whale-sized account may bring greater prosperity and stability to your company. In making that hunt, however, you also know the risk of humiliation and hunger if the hunt fails. Yet like the Inuit, you accept the burden of producing a harvest sufficient to sustain your village for the seasons to come.

We have come to know, respect, and appreciate the Inuit and their wisdom. The Inuit's reverence for the whale has profoundly influenced our thinking. To equate a whale with an exceptionally large account, as we do, is to see the analogy dissipate if, at the end of the story, the whale is dead. But we discovered in the Inuit belief system some important understandings about the whale, the village, and the gods who oversee and bless the transactions. Most importantly, the whale was not prey; rather, it was a treasured gift from the gods to ensure the survival of the village. When the villagers respectfully preserved the whale's head and returned that head to the sea, they believed that the whale would be reborn.

Whale hunting is not a parable or a fairy tale. It is the true story of how people of indomitable spirit set out with rudimentary tools to capture the largest creature on earth to ensure that their village survived and thrived.

Join us now as we embark on a whale hunt. You and your company will never be the same. We guarantee it.

Tom Searcy and Barbara Weaver Smith
Founders, The Whale Hunters®
Indianapolis, Indiana

Acknowledgments

YOU DON'T HUNT WHALES ALONE. And you don't bring books to life alone, either. As you will read, the last phase of whale hunting is to celebrate—not yourself, but the whale. We celebrate the determination, energy, and unfailing good humor of our colleagues, our customers, and our publishing team:

Bob Bonebrake, part-time whale hunter, who translated our vision into words the first time around.

The *Whale Hunters* writing team: Dr. Wynola Richards, Tim Searcy, and Don Searcy, for their contributions to whale hunting content, editorial advice, and case study write-ups.

Our subject matter experts, the extraordinary men and women who have engaged us in their business growth and who have graciously assisted us in writing about their hunts: Jack Burns, SGI; Wil Davis and Don Engel, Ontario Systems; Dan Delfino, Power Direct; Cathy Langham, Langham Logistics, Inc.; Dan Liotti, Midwest Mole; Chip McLean, Six Disciplines Leadership Center of Central Indiana; Kingdon Offenbacker, Echo Supply; Kathy

Reehling, Crew Technical Services; Rob Simmons and Rebecca Bush, Machine Specialties; Steve Walker, Walker Information; Patricia White, WorkPlace Media.

Keith McFarland, founder of McFarland Strategy Partners, who introduced us into the publishing world.

Esmond Harmsworth, world-class agent, who believed in our story and encouraged us to tell it straight; Laurie Harting, acquisitions editor, who turned a manuscript into a book; Dave Cedrone, illustrator.

Our mentors: Dan Sullivan, founder and CEO of the Strategic Coach, Inc.; Al Paison, founder of Loyalty Research and chair of an Indianapolis TEC/Vistage group; Dr. Tom Hill, founder of the Eagle Institute.

And to the many harpooners, shamans, and subject matter experts from our client companies who have helped us bring whale hunting to life through their enthusiasm to learn our process, their exuberant critique, and their grace under the pressure of sales complexity and rapid business growth.

Author Biographies

TOM SEARCY IS A NATIONALLY recognized expert and leading authority on fast-growth companies and large account sales. By the time he had turned 40, Tom had driven meteoric growth for four companies, skyrocketing their annual revenues from $15 million to $100-plus million—and, in all four cases, successful IPOs. Among these is Transcom, an international customer relationship management company with operations worldwide, for which Tom served as president and CEO. There, he engineered the fastest start-up in teleservices industry history, and in the process, earned a top-10 ranking among teleservices organizations globally and a Gold Award for Quality.

All told, Tom Searcy has commandeered over $2 billion in new business for his clients and other companies using The Whale Hunters Process™, orchestrating and closing sales to such whale-sized customers as AT&T, AOL, BMG, Disney, Sprint, UPS, Xerox, and many more.

Building on this dynamic history of managing and facilitating quick and massive growth, Tom founded The Whale Hunters to bring to fast-growing companies his intimate knowledge of the methods that can be used to land and harvest deals that are 10 to 20 times greater than their current average deal.

Through The Whale Hunters, Tom has combined into one process his knowledge and understanding of industry growth, his mastery of the intricate relationships among sales and operations personnel, and his ability to generate solid and long-lasting growth for companies. Tom serves as key business strategist for The Whale Hunters.

Trusted advisor to businesses, academic institutions, and not-for-profits alike, Dr. Barbara Weaver Smith is the inventor of ACT-Five™, an organizational change management process based on a culture of collaboration rather than internal competition. A highly respected and seasoned leader, Barbara has used this process to manage more than 50 complex collaborative projects across sectors, successfully uniting such strange bedfellows as educators, economic developers, business executives, and foundation leaders to produce social benefit and economic impact. ACT-Five™ is the basis for culture change in The Whale Hunters Process™.

Barbara takes the lead in brand management, product creation, and event design for The Whale Hunters. She specializes in helping companies to develop the fast-growth culture that whale hunting demands. Barbara is also president of Smith Weaver Smith, a consulting and project management firm specializing in strategic planning and the management of complex joint ventures. She has been a successful entrepreneur/business owner for 12 years.

Prior to launching these two companies, Barbara served as president and CEO of the Indiana Humanities Council; and, during 10 years at Ball State University, held dual appointments as professor of English and dean of the University College. She holds a PhD in English from Ball State University and is a graduate of the Institute for Educational Management at Harvard University and a master's level graduate of The Strategic Coach™.

1

The Whale Hunters' Story

COME WITH US TO A PLACE THAT is much darker, much colder, and much more dangerous than wherever you are right now. We are in the far Northwest, along the coast of Alaska, centuries ago. Imagine that along that coast you live in an earthen hut with your close family group of about 30 people. The hut is only 50 feet long and 20 feet wide. There are no windows and there are no doors. Only a few small holes in the ceiling release the smoke from the whale oil lamps that light and heat our space. To come in and out of this space, we crawl through a tunnel in the floor, out toward the coast. We have reinforced our tunnel with the rib cage bones of a whale.

We are not the only hut along this stretch of the coastline. Several other family huts make up our village. But everyone, in every hut, is doing what we are doing.

Waiting.

We have been waiting since we heard the very first pop, exploding like gunfire, letting us know with a roar that the ice floes are beginning to thaw and spring is near. We have been waiting through the long, dark winter. We have been waiting since the Northern Lights have started to fade and we approach more than four hours of daylight.

In our huts, at the earliest signs of spring, we are waiting for the whales. Every year from late winter to early spring, the whales migrate from far south of us, in what today is Baja, California, to places a little farther north than our village. As they come closer to our village, as they come nearer to the coast, we will hunt them.

Scouting the Whale

Although we know the time of year, we don't know exactly when the whales are coming. So our village sends out scouts. Every boy between the ages of seven and twelve is dispatched along the coast for miles. Well before dawn and long after dusk, the scouts look for the signs of a whale. Every man who is out hunting for caribou, anyone who is fishing in a kayak, is looking out across the coast to see the "whale sign."

It is a difficult place to spot whales. There are few hours of sunlight in a day. The water appears gray. The sky is gray. The land around us is gray. And we are looking for whales. They are gray, too.

You are probably wondering why it would be hard to spot the largest mammal on earth; and probably you have in your mind a picture of a whale spouting or breaching. But if our first glimpse of the whale is when it expels air and water through its blowhole, or when it propels its entire body wholly above the water, we are already too late. It will take too long to launch a boat and catch a whale at this point in its migration. The whales will be way beyond a point where we can catch them. Our scouts need to look for the signs of the whales before they are visible.

Our scouts know that the first sign of whales is the flocks of birds that precede them. The birds feed on the small fish that are swimming north as part of their migration. The small fish are chased by larger fish and still larger fish. Finally will come the whales.

In our village, everyone awaits the news of whale sign. One morning, a boy runs into the village, electrifying us with the news, "I have the whale sign."

Hunting the Whale

You are the harpooner. As the captain of your boat, you rally your shaman and six other oarsmen to lift the boat and launch. Your boat is called an *umiak*. It is 36 feet long, made of cypress wood, and covered in sealskin. That boat is sacred, as is everything related to the whale hunt. It's all been scrubbed down with fresh water from a river some distance away from the village—the boat, the tackle, the harpoon, the line, everything—so as to keep it pure and clean.

Everything that touches the water for the hunt, everything that touches the whale, must be pure, to observe the tradition of our ancestors.

Now we lift the boat from all sides and launch it into the water. At the front, you sit as the harpooner responsible for directing the boat close to the whale. In the back is the shaman, our spiritual leader, who provides for everyone the tradition and history. The shaman knows which chants to sing, which poems to recite, and which practices to follow to ensure that we have a safe and success-ful whale hunt.

There are six oarsmen in our boat as well. Each crew member has dual responsibilities: one, to row the boat and, two, to serve the hunt. One minds the tackle. Another minds the line. Several fish and prepare food along the journey. The hunt will take weeks out on the open water, and there is much work to accomplish along the way.

Finally, we spot a whale. The harpooner's job is to direct the boat as close as possible to the whale. Perhaps you can imagine hurl-ing your harpoon toward the whale. But that's a fiction. A 60-pound harpoon would bounce off 100,000 pounds of blubber. We need to get right next to the whale—even jump on top of the whale. And, as harpooner, you have to drive that harpoon in at just the right spot. You have been practicing all winter for just this moment. And you are successful. Your harpoon penetrates deep into the whale's blubber, and your *umiak* is now connected to the whale by a strong line made to withstand the wild and dangerous ride ahead.

Now the whale will do one of three things. It might pull away from the coastline and head deep into the ocean, taking us on a two- to four-day ride in and out of darkness, in and out of ice floes, in a very dangerous place and at a great distance from our village.

Or the whale might dive as deep as 650 feet down into the water. And it can wait, silently, as long as four hours. When it surfaces, it can emerge straight up under our boat, dislodging us. But if you are very skillful, and have put your harpoon in exactly the right place, the whale will pull toward the coastline and run along the coast until it tires. On that four-day run, everyone on the boat has a job. Tending the line is critical. If you let out the line too fast, the whale can get free. If you let it out too slowly, the boat may go under, or the line will break. Anyone who gets tangled in the line will be pulled overboard.

Finally, the whale tires. We pull the boat next to the whale and dispatch it. There is still one more job for a crew member. He needs to jump over the side, into the frigid waters, and sew the whale's mouth shut. If the mouth is left open, the whale fills with water and sinks to the bottom.

Now we must bring this whale to shore. The odds are not in our favor: a 100,000-pound whale against a 3,500-pound boat. Hauling the whale against the tide does not work. Rather, we have to work with the natural forces, the wind and the tide, to steer the whale and beach it.

While we are bringing in the whale, our young scouts are watching the coast to spot our boat. When they see us, they run back to the village to point out where the whale will be beached.

Harvesting the Whale

Everyone in the village heads to the coast as fast as possible. They bring sleds, buckets, and pots. The same tides, the same winds that brought in our whale can take it back out. Left in the open air, the whale will begin to rot. We need to harvest it quickly.

Once the whale has been beached and secured, the entire community helps with the harvest. From the age of four on, everyone has a job. At four, the children learn to harvest the whale oil from the blubber. Later, they are taught how to harvest the blubber and the skin and the meat. Eventually, they learn to handle the bone. We use every part of the whale, except for its head.

The head is preserved and kept free. When the harvest is over, the boat sets out one more time. It takes the whale's head back out to sea, where it will sink deep within the ocean and be reborn. Our village does not see the whale as a victim of our hunt. Rather, it is a gift from the gods sent to sustain us.

The leaders decide which parts of the whale go to which members of the village. The food is divided based on each one's contribution to the hunt and what the village needs for the coming year.

After all has been divided, we return to our village for a great celebration. But we do not celebrate the great hunters. We do not celebrate the boat or even the harpooner. The celebration is for the whale. The whale is what gives us life and the opportunity to thrive.

Why do we endure such difficulty and danger to hunt whales? People have been killed hunting whales in this manner, century after century. But when we hunt walrus or caribou, seals or a string of fish, we can eat only for a day or a week or two.

A whale can feed our entire village for a year.

2

Signs of the Times

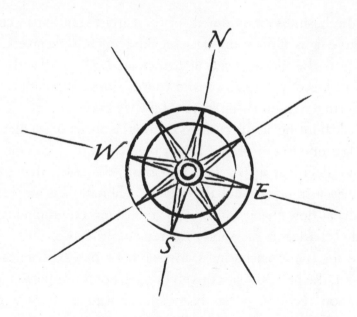

THE ANCIENT INUIT KNEW EXACTLY THE RIGHT TIME TO HUNT WHALES. It was spring. The ice was breaking. The whales were moving north through the body of water now known as the Bering Sea. We can well imagine that whale hunters wished the whales would move in

July or August when the days were never-ending and the temperatures were balmy. Driven by forces beyond their control or knowledge, however, the whales moved during the time when the wind was treacherous, the temperatures below freezing, the ice floes moving erratically, the waves mountainous, and the daylight sharply limited. And so year after year, the Inuit braved these conditions and hunted the whales because it was the right time to do so.

Today's businesspeople do not have such obvious, unmistakable signs of the correct times to shift their company's focus from smaller accounts to those 10 to 20 times larger. But if you know where to look, you will see indications that whale hunting should be on your agenda.

In the business environment of the early twenty-first century, we observe signs of the spring's ice breaking in multiple layers. Ice is breaking at the global level, at a societal level, and within the smaller realms of your industry and your business. Whales are moving. It is time to hunt them. Here is how we know.

Whale hunting, in the business context, is all about smaller companies learning to sell and to deliver big deals with big companies, which we define as *whales*. It is important, therefore, that smaller companies first understand the whales' habitat. We are looking especially at how changes in the global business environment have mandated changes in sales and procurement processes.

The international business environment has experienced sea changes in the past 30 years, driven by a host of interrelated factors. Information technology has been and continues to be a prime mover of these changes, creating a new set of both problems and opportunities for big companies, including such diverse issues as financial stress, just-in-time (JIT) inventory, quality control, and consumer capabilities. Let's look briefly at how these factors have affected how whale-sized companies do business with their suppliers, beginning with the concept of JIT.

Changing Business Environment

JIT was first articulated by Henry Ford, as described in his *My Life and Work* (Doubleday, Page & Co., Garden City, NY, 1922). It did not become part of business culture, however, until the 1950s when Toyota Motor Corporation of Japan adopted and publicized the practice as an answer to its limited access to capital. In the United States, financial stress provided the impetus to adopt JIT. Traditionally, manufacturers had stockpiled inventories and recorded them as assets on the balance sheet. But that view of warehoused inventories as assets began to change in the 1970s and 1980s. The cash invested in large inventories put a drag on a company's financial well-being, as did costs for space, utilities, and insurance. In some cases, parts were becoming obsolete before they could be sold. Financial managers and stockholders began applying pressure to business executives to find a better way to manage availability of parts. One solution was to move products back into suppliers' warehouses and order them when they were needed.

The concept of just-in-time inventory is simple and can be summed up in a few words: having the right product in the right place at the right time and in the exact amount required. Its implementation, however, is not so simple. Once the major manufacturers (whales) emptied their warehouses of inventory, suppliers (smaller companies) were left with the task of having enough material on hand to meet demands—but not so much that the bottom line of their balance sheets became skewed. Suppliers were accustomed to a process of producing goods, sending them to a warehouse, and being paid on delivery. This business model transition required them to rethink their entire business. Instead of setting their own timetables for delivery and payment for goods, they had to cut back on their production but be meticulous about the quality of everything they produced. They had to store any surplus goods themselves. And, of course, since they didn't get paid until the goods were needed, they had to develop new processes that ensured an intricate system of timing, quality, and pricing.

Demand for quality increased dramatically when supplies of any goods were sharply limited. Under the previous model, another item was available in the vast warehouses of parts. But with the implementation of this model, every part had to be precisely correct so that it could be sold and paid for on demand. New technology systems were developed to meet these demands, intricate systems that followed an item from the original request for proposal (RFP) or order through its delivery to the manufacturer. Quality control activities, many based on statistical models, were required at each step of manufacturing.

Information technology introduced more than just sophisticated inventory management systems. It opened the door to a world of information that few business leaders had previously imagined. Whereas whale-sized companies knew about a handful of vendors before, now they could find information on the Internet about hundreds of vendors around the world. End-use consumers could choose from a multitude of companies, rather than just those in close physical proximity. One size no longer fit all. If the manufacturer did not produce the product as desired, the end customer went elsewhere. An age of consumer-driven business possibilities had begun.

Information—and its use, storage, and owner—became a saleable good in itself. Companies that developed systems to obtain, control, and disseminate information were in great demand. Manipulating information became a major business. Consider, for example, the history of the airline industry. For many years, very little money has been made from the physical act of transporting passengers from one place to another. It is the companies that manage the information and reservations systems that are making real money.

All of these complex issues made a dramatic impact on large manufacturers and their suppliers. Both were forced to adopt new processes and attitudes and learn new ways to work together profitably. Gone were the days when a major manufacturer produced widgets in one size and color only; had rigidly structured processes for every conceivable activity; finalized deals one on one in the proverbial smoky room; organized departments in such a way that only members had access to the department's knowledge; and stockpiled inventory, hoarded all the engineers, and relied on one person in accounting for all financial information. Gone were the days when a supplier produced parts in advance of demand and was paid immediately for them; was haphazard about quality of materials or parts, because more were readily available; and could rely on 5- to 10-year contracts.

Perhaps one of the greatest differences experienced by companies was the change in the organization and structure of the business itself. The emphasis on quality demanded interaction among employees that had not been present before. The product development cycle had to include representatives of many departments: financial, information technology, operations, human resources, and engineers. Yet the highly developed silos of the twentieth-century corporation, based on concepts of specialization, were ineffective at meeting the new demands of the marketplace. *Transparency, collaboration,* and *quality control* were the new buzzwords of business activity.

Impact on Small Business Sales

So how does this history impact today's small to midsize company that wants to achieve rapid and sustainable growth? The companies that supply products and services to whales have changed dramatically in order to accommodate fluctuating requirements of their whale-sized customers. But the one area in which suppliers have not adjusted to participate fully in the current environment is sales. Too many suppliers rely on methods that have been used for decades, methods that do not work in the ocean of whales they wish to hunt. Let's look at some signs that your oceans have changed and your whales have adopted new ways of buying.

As the Inuit had signs of approaching whales every spring, small companies wishing to grow have signs that indicate it is time to hunt whales. As your company grows beyond a certain level, it will attract different competitors, and you will discover that whales have unique buying habits that you did not previously understand. Here are some examples:

- *New faces.* You are finding new competitors, smaller lesser-known firms, for the opportunities that you are pursuing. The newcomers seem agile and fast.
- *Thunder without rain.* You are swamped by what seem to be new RFPs, and while you have made your way onto the list of

qualified companies that bid out large business, you remain too small to win. You frequently come in second.

- *Red flags*. Bigger players are moving into your niche and, perhaps, claiming it. As you try to grow, you attract the attention of larger competitors that previously ignored you.
- *Bobbing in the ocean*. Your annual revenues go up and down like a buoy, over several years. You perceive a ceiling of revenue that you cannot break through. You are at the mercy of the sales ocean, rather than steering your way through it.
- *Trading places*. Your company is losing large accounts at a rate similar to the rate it is adding new ones.

Perhaps you have reacted to these signs by restructuring your organizational chart, hoping for greater productivity, or have replaced or reassigned staff members you consider to be your least-effective performers. You may have considered or completed acquisitions or mergers in order to achieve size, capital, and leverage. Perhaps you are developing a new product you hope will be attractive to buyers. Or maybe you are expanding into markets in which you currently have little presence. All these options sound attractive, but they demand significant financial investment; they require a marked distraction from your current client base, and based on business statistics, they have a low probability of success.

Another option is whale hunting—the organized and process-driven effort to seek, hunt, and harvest major accounts from companies that are much larger than yours. Whale hunting differs from a traditional sales approach. It works by understanding the complexity of the modern sales process and using it to the advantage of both buyer and seller.

Is Whale Hunting for You?

If your company can meet the following requirements, you might be a candidate for whale hunting.

- *Leadership will focus the entire company.*
- *People will learn new roles and pursue them effectively.*
- *You are willing to prepare extensively.*
- *You will manage your sales process aggressively.*
- *You will no longer tolerate the uncertainty of traditional sales efforts.*

Whale hunting is not for every company. It will reshape the culture of your company. But it is worth it—if you want rapid and sustained growth.

Single buyers no longer drive the buying process of a large company alone. And single sellers are no longer effective in dealing with a complex team of buyers, including technological, financial, and operations managers. Even a team of salespeople cannot be as effective as a team of people composed of representatives from many areas of your business, all focused intently on the task of whale hunting. The executives of whale-sized companies know that every major decision they make has a downstream impact, with little margin for error and little time for recovery. Selecting suppliers is one of the most significant decisions a whale-sized company can make.

The Buyers' Table

What has changed about your approach? Consider your role as the lead salesperson, the sales manager, and/or the CEO of a smaller company making a pitch to a large company. Think about this scenario:

The ultimate decision maker of a whale's buying group sits at the table with seven members of his or her buying team—people who are wondering if this prospective new supplier (your company) can provide the goods or services they need, in the right place, at the right time, of exemplary quality, and do it better than the current supplier. They are also worried about how much of a disruption you—as a new supplier—will cause in their daily way of doing business. The people at the buyers' table may represent business development, IT, operations, engineering, R&D, human resources, finance—any and all of the people who will feel the downstream impact of this transaction. All have a stake in what is happening at the table, and all are prepared to reject you at the earliest possible suggestion that all of their needs will not be met.

But as a smaller company supplier, you present a surprise to the whale's buying group. You have brought your own team to the table—your IT representatives, operations people, engineers, human resources person, chief financial officer, banker, customer services manager. Your team is thoroughly prepared. You have studied the whale company from every angle; every tough question they ask, you can answer promptly, fully, and with confidence. Each member of your team speaks directly, eloquently, and appropriately about his or her role in delivering the products and services. You assure the buying group that you will not disrupt the whale-sized company in the transition between suppliers. You allay all of their fears and concerns. The decision to give you a contract becomes easier.

If you do not see yourself and your company as the supplier in that scenario, then perhaps you are not currently selling in a way that is appropriate for the complexity of the modern whale's system of buying. You are not hunting whales. Hunting whales is not simply a matter of having a superior product, system, or service, although those are certainly important components. Whale-sized companies are equally interested in the effects that using you as a supplier will have on the entire company, the downstream impact. You have to prove to them that you and your team can deliver on a product or service that will improve their ability to do what they do best, without making any waves or causing any problems. They want improvement disguised in the cloak of "business as usual."

The truth is that whale-sized companies would love to do business with smaller suppliers. The relationship is more immediate in every way. Small suppliers can deliver goods more quickly than larger ones. It's much easier to get the CEO of a small supplier on the phone for discussion of the transactions. Small suppliers are more flexible. So why are so many small companies unsuccessful in entering this larger arena? Because they do not fully understand the fears of whale-sized companies, fears that have arisen because of all the factors affecting business during the last few decades. It may be true that you have prepared yourself and your company to respond to the immediate demand for an excellent product. We call this demand the "whale's pain." But fear trumps pain every time. If you don't know how to understand and allay the whale's fear, you will not be able to make the sale. In this book, we fully analyze our point of view about the fears of a whale (big company) and the advantages of a small company seeking to sell and service whale accounts.

The Whale Hunters' Process

The Whale Hunters' Process, though based on time-honored premises, is a revolutionary sales process that works. It understands and embraces the complex nature of whale-sized companies. It makes use of all the elements that make single selling a losing proposition. It sets out a replicable process that enables small to midsize companies and individual producers to know their whales and how best to scout, hunt, and harvest them.

In the upcoming chapters of this book, we explain in detail the Whale Hunters' Process. First, we describe the whale hunt from the perspective of the actions taken by the Inuit, because they serve so well as a workable analogy for the tasks ahead of your company, and the rewards that are available to you. Second, we apply the Inuit whale hunting practice to modern business. Through extensive examples and cases, we connect the principles and practices of the Inuit to a comparable set of relevant principles and practices to guide a modern-day business "whale hunt."

The Whale Hunters' Process is based on a nine-phase model, illustrated here. It is a stable model that we have applied successfully to a wide range of companies, industries, and sales practitioners.

We define nine phases of the Whale Hunters' Process, each of which must be performed with care for the process to be successful. These phases are clustered into three primary stages of activity called *scout*, *hunt*, and *harvest* the whales.

Each of the nine phases itself comprises a number of steps. The definition, importance, and complexity of each step are determined by the whale hunting team, or company. In other words, the model is translated into a specific map for a specific company.

Each of the subsequent chapters provides guidance, insight, and examples of how to apply these steps to your own sales process. As you read, imagine your company as a village, all of whose members are setting out with a single goal in mind: to harvest the whale and partake of the bounties it can offer.

Scout the Whale

The three phases of scouting are *know*, *seek*, and *harpoon* the whale. Harpooning the whale, the last of these, indicates that a year's worth of preparation went into every action that preceded that dramatic penetration of the whale's blubber.

Know the Whale

During the long, dark, bitterly cold months of winter in Alaska, the village concentrated on getting to know the whale that they would capture and harvest in the spring. They discussed the hunt of the previous year, pointing out what went right and what went wrong. They decided on the oarsmen who would accompany the shaman and the harpooner in the umiak when they launched it. They analyzed the abilities of each of the oarsmen, and pictured, in great detail, how each would respond in emergencies. Perhaps they changed their minds many times about the capabilities of individual oarsmen as they set about to form the strongest team, not the strongest individuals. They told stories about the great hunts of the past, celebrating the years when weather was smooth, the whale was unusually large, and the entire hunt was without incident. They mourned the years when the whale capsized the umiak, and both whale and fellow villagers were lost. They planned for every contingency they could imagine and then tried to imagine even more. They discussed how whales move in the water and how to get the umiak close to the whale without being capsized by its thrashing tail. They discussed weather, and thought of new ways to combat or endure it. They talked about the differences among whales and how to spot the one whale that would be theirs.

Whales migrate in pods, some as small as 3 or 4 members and some as large as 40 to 100. In the Bering Sea, many different types of baleen whales migrated, so knowing which type of whale was to be hunted was essential. Not only could ancient hunters predict the size of the pod but also its movement. Some whale pods move more slowly than others. The quickest can go the equivalent of 30 miles per hour. Some whales float after being killed, making the homeward trek much easier. The most successful whale hunts culminated in a very large, slow-moving whale that floated after it died. But finding that particular whale took knowledge and determination.

Whale hunters learned, and taught their children, which whales were which. They learned how to identify them by speed, size of pod, color, length of time spent under water, amount and intensity of noises made, number of blowholes, and the depth at which they swam. They learned to tell the females from the males (females are usually larger and, therefore, more desirable) and identify any calves that were swimming near their mothers. They knew that the bond between mother and calf is especially strong, and that bond made a female especially dangerous.

The harpooner honed his weapon, strengthened his body, and prepared his umiak for the hunt. He knew the challenge of hitting the exact spot at the right time under the tenuous conditions of the moving umiak, the thrashing whale, and the treacherous weather.

By the time that the villagers heard the first signs of breaking ice, they had an indelible image of the whale they wanted and how they would carry out the hunt. They knew their whale.

Seek the Whale

Responsibility for the vital scouting task rested with the village shaman and his trained helpers, the scouts. Scouts, usually boys between the ages of seven and twelve, had been taught since they were three or four the signs that indicated whales were moving.

In the best cases they saw the evidence of approaching whales well before the big animals arrived. They knew that small fish and krill (a shrimplike invertebrate animal) were the standard diet for whales. Of course, the fish and krill were not visible from the shoreline, so the scouts watched for other predators that also favored that particular diet, such as easily identifiable birds and smaller sea predators like dolphins. A school of dolphins accompanied by a flock of birds was a fairly positive indicator that whales would be following shortly.

Because of their age, level of experience, and lack of physical strength, the young scouts were low in the village hierarchy when it came to hunting. But in terms of their training and their acute powers of observation, they were unparalleled in the village.

Although the scouts were seldom also oarsmen in the umiak, their job was one of the most important to the hunt, and was so recognized by the village. They were intelligence gatherers, the village's eyes and ears. If the scouts were successful, the village had enough time to launch the boat and begin the pursuit. If they were unsuccessful and missed the early signals of whales, then the village would not have the time needed to successfully catch up with the whales, resulting perhaps in starvation for the village.

Harpoon the Whale

Since the harpooner was the captain of the boat, and the one responsible for actually harpooning the whale, he made the decision about the right time to do so. Many conditions had to be exactly right for his success. The umiak had to be steady, and it had to move at the same pace as the whale being targeted. If the hunters were targeting a female with a calf, they had to make sure that the calf did not interrupt their operation. They had to stay away from the middle of the pod, or their umiak might capsize. Chances were great that the seas were rough, the wind was bellowing, and ice or snow was blowing in the harpooner's face as he stood ready to strike. And given the fact that April in the Bering Sea brings daylight for fewer than five hours a day, it was probably dark.

Add to that the fact that the harpooner had to strike in exactly the right place on the whale for success, and the risks become even more acute. He had to strike where the harpoon could sink into the blubber without hitting any bones, or his harpoon would not withstand the rough ride ahead. He couldn't strike too far back on the whale for fear its tail would thrash around and capsize the boat. Typically, the harpooner would transport himself from the umiak to the whale's back in order to plant the harpoon; he didn't just hurl the harpoon from a distance. When the harpoon was placed, he had to deftly reclaim his space in the umiak.

Once the harpooner had struck, the oarsmen had to do two things simultaneously: they had to steer out of the whale's way as it thrashed in the water, and they had to secure the line attached to the harpoon and now embedded deep into the whale's blubber. But one of the most difficult and painstakingly precise parts of the entire hunt was now behind them. They had harpooned the whale.

Hunt the Whale

The hunting stage refers to the most dangerous activities of the whale hunt: *ride, capture,* and *sew* the whale. These tasks required the utmost strength and dedication on the part of all the Inuit oarsmen.

Ride the Whale

The harpoon did not kill the whale, which reacted instantly to the weapon being thrust into its body by trying to get rid of it. The only way it knew to do that was to dive or swim. The oarsmen were hoping that swimming would be the chosen option, since diving would certainly mean capsizing and icy death. Depending on the length of the rope connecting the harpoon and the umiak, the whale diving could pull the boat under with it. Barring that, the whale could come up for air directly under the boat, throwing it and its occupants into the air and then into the frigid waters.

The whale might swim at top speed out into the open sea. If that was the path it chose, all the oarsmen could do was hang on as tightly as possible. Lashed by the wind and sea, their hands blistered and sore, the salt water aggravating their open wounds, the oarsmen had to maintain the right amount of tension on the rope as the whale towed them along. If the rope got too tight, the whale could break free. If it got too loose, the whale could turn suddenly and attack the umiak.

This danger-filled ride could last for days, depending on the whale's endurance. The jagged edges of the moving ice floes could slam into the umiak, so the oarsmen had to steer as deftly as possible while being dragged. Their ability to withstand these elements is almost unimaginable. Yet they did so. They rode the whale.

Capture the Whale

At some point, the whale tired of the fight and began to slow down. The hunters would try to maneuver the whale so that it was headed for the coastline, but often those efforts were in vain. The whale was exhausted but not yet dead. It could still get a burst of energy and start the chase over again. So the oarsmen knew not to let their vigilance wane. The whale was most at home in the deepest parts of the Bering Sea and would head there if possible. And the oarsmen continued to try to control the direction and force of the whale's momentum. Eventually, the whale ceased to swim forward, at which point the hunters knew that they had captured the whale.

Sew the Mouth Shut

Now came the most fascinating and most dangerous of jobs connected with the entire whale hunt. The oarsmen steered the umiak next to the whale's mouth and its 350 to 400 baleen plates, each up to 9.5 inches long. They assumed that the whale was either dead or near death, but could not know for sure. One oarsman would slip out of the umiak, into the icy water, and swim up next to the whale's mouth. Then he would sew that mouth shut. If he did not do this, the mouth would fill with water and the whale would sink to the bottom and be lost. The whale might be miles from the coastline, but its mouth was now sewn shut.

Harvest the Whale

The final stage in the Whale Hunters' Process is harvesting the whale, which consists of three phases: *beach, honor,* and *celebrate* the whale. These phases involve the entire village, as well as those in the umiak who had hunted the whale.

Beach the Whale

Although the whale's mouth was sewn shut, the difficulties of the hunt were not over. The whale had to be directed toward shore. Given the small size of the umiak and the hugeness of the whale, towing it was out of the question. So the oarsmen had to rely on a combination of wind, waves, and tide to carry the whale in. This process might take a number of days, especially if the whale had taken the boat out into the open sea. Still contending with whatever fierce weather the April sea was sending their way, the hunters now had an additional problem. Sea and air creatures that had been ignoring them earlier were now following them, approaching closer and closer, attracted to the whale. Having a whale attached to their boat while trying to fend off predators and guide the whale to shore made the return trip seem much more difficult and tricky than the hunt. But, eventually, they began to see the outlines of the shore and, before long, the outlines of people lining it.

By the time the oarsmen were in clear view of the shore, village scouts had already announced that the hunters were returning. Soon all the villagers were there, and many waded out into the water to do their part in helping to move the whale up onto the beach.

Honor the Whale

As soon as the whale was on the beach, the job of sharing it began. Although time was of the essence and could not be wasted, many rituals were performed in honor of the whale. Everyone believed that the way the village treated this whale would predict their future success in hunting. They did not take the whale for granted. Everyone in the village had a job in harvesting this most valuable of gifts. Every part of the whale would be used in some manner, except the head which would be preserved and taken back out to sea. The work took many days as bones, blubber, skin, and meat were divided among the villagers and prepared for storage and use during the next winter.

Celebrate the Whale

After the work was complete, the entire village came together again to celebrate the whale. Music, dancing, and laughter all emanated from the large circle formed near the shoreline. Food and drink were abundant. Prayers of thanksgiving were raised for the whale that gave its life so that the village could live during the upcoming year.

Stories about the hunt were related, and everyone reveled in the return of loved ones and the bounty of the whale. Soon the cycle would begin again. But for now, the village was content.

The Village Strategy

Now you have a decision to make: Are you and your company ready to undertake a whale hunt? If you have decided not to rely solely on hunting caribou and seals during the coming year, if you have some idea of where the whales are in the vast ocean, and if your company is prepared to do the work necessary for a whale hunt, then you are ready. This is not a decision that should be made lightly or in isolation, because the hunt will be demanding, and you must be certain of a high level of commitment from others within your company.

Whale hunting is risky. If you approach the effort haphazardly, you could end up losing the deal and tarnishing your or your company's reputation far into the future. Not only are whales difficult and expensive to land, but they also require an increased level of internal attention and performance to retain. When a single new account adds 20 percent or more to gross revenue, your entire organization is significantly affected. Workloads increase, and probably you will have to hire new people. If you lose this account prematurely, the company will suffer from the loss of prestige, revenue, and, perhaps, jobs.

Landing a whale will not help a struggling company survive. Foundering, unprofitable companies will find their situations only become worse when they begin confronting whales. Difficulties within the current sales system have to be resolved *before* they begin a whale hunt.

In spite of these difficulties, however, selling to whales is good business.

- First, whale hunting saves you money over the long haul. There is a cost in time and resources for any size transaction. Many costs of sale do not increase in direct proportion to the size of the potential sale. Hunting whales will give you tremendous economies of scale.
- Second, significant brand benefits attach to your company if you list whales among your clients and customers. Hunting and harvesting whales will validate your capabilities and will attract other whales to your company.
- Third, scouting, hunting, and harvesting whales will literally transform your business. Along with the obvious benefits of more revenue and profit come increased market share, industry reputation, and the opportunity for staff growth and improved morale. Having an affiliation with a widely recognized client can also give your company greater influence over your suppliers, as well as greater significance in the eyes of your investors and backers.

When you decide that you are ready for whale hunting, you will need to understand three core principles before you begin your hunt. These principles are described next.

Whale Hunting Is 90 Percent Process and 10 Percent Magic

Entrepreneurial companies frequently try to grow based on the talents of a charismatic, instinctive salesperson, often the company owner or founder, who has a rare talent for finding and closing deals. To outsiders, this person's abilities may seem almost magical. A start-up company can be hugely successful with this "rock star" in the lead. However, as a long-term growth strategy, this technique of relying on one person does not hold up. Ultimately, magic is unpredictable, expensive, and hard to scale. Individual magic seldom works with whales, where a team approach is much preferred. As noted earlier in this chapter, successful whale hunting involves a clearly defined, nine-phase sales process that you can teach, monitor, improve, replicate, and scale. The goal is to develop a permanent asset within your company that is independent of particular individuals and that you can duplicate successfully to provide a wealth of future sales growth.

In the Inuit village, the whale hunt was so vital for survival that everyone became involved. The whale hunting process never ended. The village was always alert and working to make the next hunt successful. In the modern whale hunt, the village leaders need to share responsibility for the company's readiness to bring in and serve the new big accounts. This principle is one of the most important lessons modern fast-growth companies can learn from the Whale Hunters' Process.

Focus on the Hunt, Not the Hunter

You don't hunt whales alone. No Inuit would cast out alone into the forbidding ocean to hunt a whale. An individual or a small hunting party could pursue a caribou or walrus, but not a whale. In the same way, hunting large accounts requires a crew, a team. The lone gunman of yore, with the magic touch approach that worked for smaller accounts, does not work consistently for whale deals.

In their founding stages, most entrepreneurial companies tend to have a charismatic leader with drive and knowledge and a natural knack for closing deals. As the company grows, the founder tries to attract heroic salespeople and equip them to replicate his or her expertise. Absent the entrepreneur's unique ability, however, these salespeople often fail. In contrast, whale hunting is a collaborative leadership model. Capturing, beaching, and harvesting a whale is far too complex to be left to the expertise of a single hunter. The Inuit whale hunters learned to organize the resources of the entire village in the annual whale hunt.

Team Techniques of Whale Hunters

Do you want to develop the team techniques of the whale hunters? Ask yourself these key questions:

- *Do you focus on the hunt or the hunter?*
- *Do you send a team or an individual to capture a large account?*
- *Is your sales strategy built on process or heroics?*
- *Can you harvest—service and retain—the next whale-sized account that you capture?*

Over the centuries, Inuit whale hunters came up with the perfect combination of skill sets that has proven to also work in modern deals. The typical Inuit crew consisted of eight members, with each crewman having a clear and well-defined role in the hunt.

The Inuit shaman was the heart of the hunt. Stationed at the stern of the umiak, he listened to the wind, kept track of the shape and ferocity of the waves, read the seabird activity and stars. He knew which rituals were in order, which songs to sing, which prayers to chant during the long hunt. In the modern whale hunt, the shaman, analogous to the sales manager, is the direct supervisor of the harpooners. He or she is responsible for training the members of the boat crew and facilitating the hunting process. The shaman determines when the village will launch a boat to hunt a specific whale.

The harpooner, who was the captain and generally the owner of the umiak, is analogous to the salesperson who pursues whale-sized accounts. The harpooner directed the whale hunt. It was his job to guide the boat close enough to the whale to set the harpoon. Harpooners in the Whale Hunters' Process are responsible for identifying the key decision makers inside the prospective big accounts. They are also responsible for initially qualifying the potential whale account and generating the internal interest in the account within the selling company.

Inuit oarsmen did more than just power the boat. They kept the crew fed by fishing during the hunt. They also kept the harpoon line and the other necessary tools in shape. These oarsmen equate well to the key subject matter experts within the selling company. These individuals have specific knowledge of elements of the products and services that your company is selling. They also contribute to bringing the new account into the boat as the successful sales process ends.

Sustained Change Requires Sustained Energy

Whale hunting will require a significant change in your company's culture. When you reach a plateau in your growth—one of those turning points at which your next steps will require significant changes in your targets, your markets, and your approach to those markets—you will confront a culture crisis. Many, if not most, of the practices that have *propelled* your growth thus far represent the practices that will *keep* you at the level that you have already achieved. This understanding is a bitter pill, a hard lesson to learn. It requires inspired leadership to propel your team to a totally new level of expertise and confidence.

Prepare to invest consistent energy over at least one year's dura-tion to convert your company to a whale-hunting culture. Whale hunting is not a quick fix, a magic wand, or a training program. Rather, it is a comprehensive effort that involves all of your leader-ship team in growing your company's ability to sell and service much larger accounts.

Whale hunting is not just a trendy philosophy or sales tech-nique. It involves no clever phrases or trick questions to trap a prospect. It is instead a proven set of business processes, developed over 20 years of sales, sales management, and general business man-agement experience, greatly amplified by our understanding of the Inuit whale hunt.

Whatever business challenges you face, whatever you fear, whatever keeps you awake at night, chances are your terrain is less treacherous and your hunt less dangerous than those of the Inuit.

Signs of the Times

All the signs that we read tell us that the world of the whales has changed. Whales buy differently than they used to. They have more complex constraints in place. They have more fears. To overcome these constraints and to allay these fears, they are implementing new buying processes that require new selling processes in order to be successful.

The upcoming chapters describe in detail the capabilities that you need to develop, and the nine phases of process that you should follow, in order to thrive in the modern world of whale hunting.

3

Know the Whale

MUCH OF THE WORK OF KNOWING the whale must take place before the April launch of the boat. Thus, between the midwinter solstice and the sounds of ice breaking in the Bering Sea, the Inuit planned their upcoming hunt meticulously.

We imagine that they analyzed the villagers to determine which of them would comprise the best possible team. They had to have strong, courageous people; an excellent fisherman, who could keep the crew fed during the trip; and people who would not give up, either in spirit or strength, for the hunt would be treacherous and, perhaps, deadly. In addition, they needed someone capable of taking on the exceedingly dangerous task of sewing the whale's mouth shut. All these people had to be willing and able to work as a team under adverse conditions, and persevere in their quest for the whale. All members of the boat placed their lives in the care of the others.

The Inuit also reviewed what they knew about the ocean and the pods of whales that would be traveling toward the Arctic, and speculated whether the whales would be humpbacks, northern rights, or orcas. Each kind of whale required a different kind of hunt, so they mulled over the approach they would use for each; and within the kind, considered each individual whale, whether male or female. Maybe they discussed the pros and cons of each type of whale and then decided on the one to hunt, if the circumstances proved favorable. They talked about the various sizes of whales; how to approach a female whale with her calf at her side; which whales will float after they die, which ones tend to stick closer to shore, and which ones would provide the most meat, bone, blubber, and oil for the village. But at this point, all their discussion was a compilation of theories. They planned as fully as they could for the upcoming hunt, knowing full well that the actual circumstances might be quite different from what they envisioned. They also knew, however, that without these theories, they could not complete a hunt to its full advantage.

Because whale hunting was a sacred ritual, the Inuit and their shaman chanted, sang, and prayed as they prepared their tools and their dress. They wove the rope, and they carved the shank of the harpoon and its blade. They washed and outfitted their boat. They made a new vest and parka for every Inuit who would be on the whale hunting umiak. And throughout the long winter of preparation, they prayed and invoked the blessings of their ancestors in the human and spiritual worlds.

Chart the Waters

In the analysis we call chart the waters, these are the kinds of activities you will undertake in the first phase of whale hunting. You will analyze your company, its image, and its unique capabilities, and you will learn to chart the waters where the whales reside and to identify which whales you are going to hunt. You will get to know the kinds of whales in your particular ocean and compare their size, weight, speed, and location, just as the Inuit did. Because you have better technologies and a wider geographic scope than the Inuit, you can even choose the ocean in which you will hunt. You are not limited to the waters that flow past your village. And you will develop a ritual, a repeatable mode of preparation, to guide your hunt.

Just as the Inuit assessed the umiak crew for its strength and cohesion, you need to assess the strength and accuracy of your brand promise. What is your company's current message to the market? If you are like many entrepreneurial companies, your marketing messages might be broad and inclusive. Perhaps you identify a laundry list of the things you can do, *plus* a comprehensive inventory of the industries you serve, *plus* the kinds of customers for which your products or services are useful. It's like casting a net into the ocean to see what you can catch, and believing that whatever you catch you can make your product or service fit. Using this approach, what you will catch in your net will be other small companies. It will *never* be a whale. Capturing a big one requires a clear and concise brand promise. Here are some vague brand promises that we've observed:

- Our approach incorporates continuous program improvement through the use of effective metrics and quality reviews.
- We distinguish ourselves from our competitors with our excellence in design and our project management skills.
- Our solutions are custom designed to meet the desires of our clients. Systems are designed for ease of use regardless of the complexity of the components or the unique client needs.
- We are big enough to meet your needs yet small enough to provide personal service.

You need to avoid promises like these because, while they may be true, they *fail to differentiate your brand from any of thousands of other brands, products, and services*. You could be a hotel, a pizza parlor, a landing gear manufacturer, a software developer, a call center, a logistics expert, an insurance company, a direct marketer, and so on.

We cannot overemphasize the importance of your brand promise, that unique competitive advantage, that one thing that sets you apart from your competitors, that will make your umiak faster and more steady, your harpooner's strike more sure, and your harvest rich.

If you want to grow your company faster than your competitors, and clarify your brand promise, you must identify your markers of distinction. That navigation requires three steps:

1. Understand your ocean.
2. Define superior benefits.
3. Define unique benefits.

Understand Your Ocean

We define the ocean as your competitive environment. The ocean has market standards that all competitors know and claim to meet and exceed. Every industry has a list of benefits that each of the competitors claims. Typically, these benefits include some combination of quality, speed of delivery, innovation, and pricing. At the level where each provider makes similar claims, everyone is stuck with "assertion selling"—asserting that you are better than the other guy because you say so.

- Identify all of the claims in which you and everyone else in the ocean are similar. What are the market standards in your ocean that all competitors know and claim they do best?
- Conduct a systematic analysis of your sales and marketing materials and those of your competitors to identify these similarities.
- Study the larger competitors, whose attention you will attract when you go after bigger deals.
- Be certain you can sail in this ocean.

Define Superior Benefits

The second step is to identify those standard benefits at which you are clearly superior to your competitors. You need to identify *with* your ocean to create a common language and understanding with the whales. Big companies need to feel safe; they need to know that you have the ability to comply with their basic requirements in all areas of delivery from your company to their companies. To be successful, this is the initial level of communication. Can you meet the necessary specifications at 100 percent of standards? Surpassing all expectations for 9 out of 10 requirements will not overcome missing by even a small amount a single requirement. However, once you are able to meet all requirements of the ocean, you can choose one or two for which you can demonstrate extraordinary value and important differentiation. Lead with the common factors that you can deliver in a superior way.

Define Unique Advantage

The third and final step is to identify those true differentiating characteristics that make your product and/or service offerings unique. If the general approach in the marketplace is to standardize, show your unique ability to customize. If the standard market turnaround time is 10 weeks, emphasize your 4-week delivery. If 80 percent of the market wants cheap and easy, emphasize your ability to do that 20 percent of the most difficult work for which certain whales will pay premium prices.

One of our clients has to navigate a very crowded ocean. This company, Power Direct, is in the outsourced call center business. They provide a sales channel for their midsize and large clients that are looking to add customers through direct sales contact. More than 4,000 competitors swim in Power Direct's ocean, causing dramatic price pressure, as well as growing capacity generated from offshore competitors. Power Direct had a long list of "me-too" characteristics when measured against its competitors. High quality, good technology, great people all made the list—just as they would make the list of all of their competitors.

How did Power Direct find its brand promise? First, we helped them identify several abilities in the "me-too" list that far outpaced their competitors. Specifically, they are sales specialists (not generalists) who generate a particularly high yield in certain defined customer markets. They can prove this with historical results in comparison to competitors. Their brand promise should clarify the markets in which they outpace their competitors. Additionally, the customers they secure for their clients tend to remain as customers longer. So their brand promise should emphasize the lifetime value of a new customer. In each of these key characteristics, they perform the same services as their competitors, but they have a track record of exceeding industry standards of performance.

Next, they identified several exceptional abilities they have—capabilities that their competitors do not have at any level. In the direct sales world, the most difficult work to do is with a customer (or a particular offer from a customer) that has a low conversion rate—that is, it takes many calls to make a single sale. Perhaps these companies are selling high-priced items and/or making complex sales that require several conversations and callbacks with the same prospective buyer. Some sales require that prospects relay sensitive information over the telephone—such as date of birth, Social Security number, or annual income. Convincing people to provide personal information is difficult. Finally, situations with both low rates of sales *and* that require sensitive information gathering are troublesome. Most direct sales companies shy away from these kinds of contracts because of their difficulty. Perhaps they can staff a few people to do this work, but 20 people, 100 people? Very challenging.

In contrast to its competitors, Power Direct is especially effective in handling all of these qualities—a complex sale, a low rate of conversion, gathering sensitive information. When they identified

Table 3.1 Core Capabilities of Power Direct versus Key Competitors

Capability	Key Competitive Call Centers	Power Direct
Quality control	Above market standard	Above market standard
Up-to-date technology	Continuous upgrades	Continuous upgrades
Effective training of personnel	Extensive training	Extensive training
Metrics and timely reports	Timely reports	Timely reports
Gather sensitive information	(Not competent)	Excellent
Persistence on low-conversion calls	(Not interested)	Excellent
Success rate with complex sales	(Low)	(High)
Number of associates prepared to handle complex and difficult sales	(Fewer than 20)	(More than 200)

these core, unique capabilities (itemized in Table 3.1), their world of competition suddenly decreased from 4,000 to a handful. Certain customers will pay premium rates for this particular set of services. These are the criteria on which Power Direct will build its message to the marketplace of whales. Later, we will illustrate how this knowledge influenced their sales targets.

Know Yourself

Before you attempt to know your whales, first you have to know yourself. You need to answer some important questions about your company and your industry. You can conduct this analysis yourself, or, if you are lucky enough to have a leadership team, assemble them to work through this process. Pull together examples of your company's brochures, power points, Web site pages, and capabilities documents. Compile the messages that you are sending to your market. Are they clearly focused on a distinct market segment, or are you trying to cover all of the territory?

You know that all buyers want good value, prompt delivery, high quality, and innovative goods and services. What do you want buyers to see when they have an image of your company? What do you believe that buyers see? Ask yourself the following questions:

- Do you demand precise quality?
- Are yours the lowest available prices?
- Are you extremely efficient, offering low lead time and speedy delivery?
- Are you cutting-edge in your machinery, systems, research, and innovation?
- Are you well known within your industry?
- Do you stress honesty in all your transactions, or do you cut corners here and there?
- Do you always meet deadlines?
- Are you able to sustain long professional relationships with your buyers?

We move from the realm of what you believe or wish to be true about your company to analyzing what you know to be true and comparing the two. To find that unique competitive advantage, look first at the statistics that describe your company and then analyze what they mean.

Conduct a Market Assessment

Start with an honest self-assessment of your current marketing and sales activities. Look at solid sales data from the two most recent years, along with your projections for the upcoming year. Then determine your current ocean of whales by scrutinizing the number of accounts you have now that represent more than 5 percent of your revenue. Name those whales. This is the ocean in which you are currently hunting.

Next, identify all the components of your sales and marketing processes, gathering relevant materials for review. Your list might include the following:

- Company's branding
- Prospecting process
- Sales process
- Process for growing existing accounts
- Sales management
- Sales staff
- Sales information and materials

Next, grade your company's current sales and marketing process using the following scale, with examples to support your grading:

1 = Fatal weakness of the company

2 = Worse than competitors

3 = Same level as competitors

4 = Better than competitors

5 = Unique advantage

Finally, finish two statements about your company:

My company's biggest growth issue is _____.

The one sales area I need help with is _____.

Sales & Marketing Self-Assessment

DATA

Previous Year Sales _____

Current Year Sales _____

Next Year's Sales Projections _____

Number of accounts greater than 5% of your revenue _____

Who are your current whales?

Score your company: 1–5

1 = Company fatal weakness

2 = Wore than competitors

3 = Same level as competitors

4 = Better than competitors

5 = Unique competitive advantage

	1	2	3	4	5
Company's branding	1	2	3	4	5
Prospecting Process	1	2	3	4	5
Sales Process	1	2	3	4	5
Process for growing existing accounts	1	2	3	4	5
Sales Management	1	2	3	4	5
Sales Staff	1	2	3	4	5
Sales Information and Materials	1	2	3	4	5

Finish these statements:

1. My company's biggest growth issue is _____

_____

_____

2. The one sales area I need help with is _____

_____

Ask every member of your team who touches your sales process to answer these questions. Let the responses remain anonymous through a third party, who will compile the results. Then bring your team together to discuss your collective assessment. Learn what you know and examine what you don't know. Where do you agree about your message; on what criteria do you disagree? What do you need to learn in order to come to closer alignment? Which stakeholders (employees, advisors, customers, investors, friends) can best help you to achieve clarity on your brand promise?

All companies assume they are selling their products; but they are also selling more than that. If the production of excellent products or services was all that was important in sales, then no need would exist for a sales department. Any company could simply announce what it was producing and wait for the orders to come in. Identifying your whale begins with an effort to understand what you actually sell. What makes you different from the others in your marketplace? Why have you been successful, while others in your industry have not? Why have you been unsuccessful in some areas where your competitors have found success? And always remember that selling to whales is not the same as selling to smaller companies.

Our clients often find this exercise instructive in ways they had not glimpsed before. Perhaps your brand promise is, "We produce lightbulbs." But why do people buy your lightbulbs? Do they last longer? Are they brighter? Are they cheaper? Do they fit into fixtures for which other firms do not make bulbs? Do they consume less energy? Can you deliver them faster and more reliably than your competitors? Are you constantly pushing the edge of lightbulb research and development? These questions can help you hone your brand promise.

At this point in the process of knowing your whale, your team addresses important questions about what has made your company successful to this point, such as the following:

- Which of our products and services is the most profitable?
- In which markets have we been most successful? Will our market be larger or smaller 5 or 10 years from now?
- What are the current trends in our industry?
- What will we be selling 5 or 10 years from now?
- What makes our sale complex?
- Are we spending time on products and services that are no longer profitable? If so, why?
- What do we do better than our competitors? What do we do worse?
- What is our current most troublesome sale? Why?

You are looking for what is factually unique about your company, so these are not questions that can be answered quickly or lightly with a few brainstorming sessions. Employ the "five whys" to get beyond glib or superficial answers to the root cause. For example, perhaps your competitor is better than you in delivery time. Why? They have more raw materials on hand. Why? They anticipate the need more accurately than you do. Why? They have people devoted to researching trends in the industry, and you have none. Why? They have more money to devote to research. Why? They reorganized recently to add researchers to the team because they say anticipating trends is more important than each management person having a secretary.

This is not the time to make yourself feel good; it is a time for honesty and precision in preparation for your next steps. Whale hunting is an expensive, dangerous activity that demands precision and excellent teamwork. Your work in knowing the whale will prepare you to research and to name the specific companies that you want to identify as your whale targets.

Don't let the process of narrowing your brand promise frighten you. As you implement whale-hunting processes into your sales and business strategy, you will continue to hunt and fish along the way. You will feed your family and your village.

Whale Hunting and Wealth Management

During the process of knowing the whale, many CEO clients ask us, "How much of my business should be whale-hunting?" Our answer is another question: "How much faster than your market's rate of growth do you want to grow?" Whale hunting promises fast growth. If you want to grow faster than you have grown, if you want to grow faster than your competitors are growing, hunting whales offers a unique advantage.

Do you have friends, family members, or acquaintances who are financial planners? If so, you've undoubtedly been invited to a free seminar, with dinner at a local restaurant, where they feed you pasta and wine, then turn down the lights and turn on the slides while you struggle to stay awake. The first slide usually illustrates a balanced investment strategy, typically in the form of a pyramid, in which you would put the majority of your assets into low-risk/low-return investments, such as bonds or T-bills, and a smaller portion of assets into middle-risk/middle-return investments, such as mutual funds or blue chip stocks, and only a very small portion of assets into high-risk/high-return investments, such as REITs.

We think the same strategy works for whale hunting, as our wealth pyramid illustrates:

Wealth Pyramid

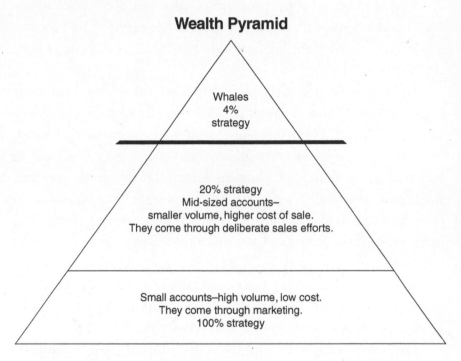

Whales
4%
strategy

20% strategy
Mid-sized accounts–
smaller volume, higher cost of sale.
They come through deliberate sales efforts.

Small accounts–high volume, low cost.
They come through marketing.
100% strategy

At the bottom of this pyramid are low-risk, low-return investments that chug along without a lot of ups or downs in their returns. Think of these as your routine branding and marketing activities. Your marketing efforts to locate these accounts are broad-based messages, offered up to 100 percent of the universe of your potential customers. At this level, you use marketing tactics to bring people *to you*. Tools include Web sites, trade shows, brochures—you put stuff out there and hope that the phone will ring. At this level you may be sending out proposals and even quotes that are not strategic to your business, which is another term for "free consulting." You are telling the marketplace your baseline price and deliverables. These messages go to your current customers, who don't need them; to your competitors, who you don't want to see them; and to prospects you don't want to hear from. The best you can hope to do with this method is to meet the growth rate of your marketplace.

The middle portion of the pyramid has more fluctuation but offers higher returns. These are midrisk, midreturn investments, accounts that you acquire through direct sales efforts or through a sales channel. You are deliberately selling *to them*. You have a sales force whose members go on a strategic planning retreat, off-site, to do creative, intelligent, thoughtful work for the purpose of picking some 20 percent of your market as targeted prospects upon which to focus. You prospect, you knock on doors, you make cold calls, you network—and you will generally see a 10 to 25 percent conversion rate. And if you execute this strategy well—with good people and good planning—you will be successful. Over time, sustained selling excellence at this level can deliver a rate of growth that is twice the market rate.

To recap, your growth with these two strategies will be near the market rate of growth for your industry. In other words, you will grow with the economy. With traditional marketing and follow-up efforts, if you are very successful, you will grow at the average growth of your market. If you are great at execution, and implement a focused sales strategy, you may achieve twice the market rate of growth. And you can sustain such success for as long as three to five years. But there is a financial cap, a glass ceiling, to these strategies. The cost of goods sold, the reasonable profit margin that your company will take, will leave you only a certain amount of money to invest in future growth. Your investments are unlikely to exceed what your competitors are investing. You will hover at the norm.

To get past these economics you have to hunt whales. For the whale hunting component of your business, you can focus on only 4 percent of the marketplace—a strategically identified list of prospects that are perfect for you. Of course, your sales and marketing teams are already fully engaged in carrying out the first two strategies. So who will hunt the whales? The executive management team! And if you are gong to involve the executive team, you will need to have a close rate better than 50 percent in order to recoup your sales investment. So you will need a clear system, a tightly defined list of prospects, and a very predictable close ratio.

The best way to increase your close ratio is to decrease the denominator—hunt a lot fewer whales. Do not focus on how to close more whales, but on how to hunt fewer. The upcoming chapters will show you how to define perfect whales for your company and how to close more than 50 percent of the deals you pursue.

The apex of the pyramid is the high-risk and high-reward segment of your strategy. Whale hunting happens at this level.

We've drawn a line between the middle point and the high point in the investment pyramid. Everything below this line will grow your business at a market standard for growth in your industry, where your competitors are achieving the same levels of growth that you are, by doing the same things you are doing. Like you, your competitors are taking positive steps to improve sales, such as:

- Beefing up the sales staff—swapping out low performers for higher performers.
- Betting on sales management—hiring a business development manager.
- Implementing sales tools—CRM, contact management, sales kits, and demos.

■ Buying sales training—investing in the performance of your current sales personnel.

In this universe, you will achieve some incremental advantage for a while. Then your competitors will pass you for a while. Back and forth it will go, each of you achieving a bigger or smaller slice of the standard market pie. Whale hunting is the only way to grow your business aggressively *above the market rate*.

If you choose to become a whale hunter, you will leave your competitors wading in the low tide. You will be riding the big waves because you will learn how to perform the following activities:

1. Set the rate of "market rate plus" growth by defining in advance what size accounts you want to hunt and how much business you want from them. We call that process *Chart the waters*.
2. Develop an investment strategy to allocate your resources to achieve the amount of growth you want. You will balance your business with small and midsize accounts to support your market rate growth while you hunt whales to fuel your maximum growth potential. We call that process *Plan the hunt*.
3. Predict with greater accuracy the speed of business acquisition, plotting a longer-range growth strategy. We call that process *Manage the hunt*.
4. Develop a process to maximize the opportunities from your current whales, about which you know more. You can balance your risk appetite with knowledge so that your whale growth is less risky. We call that process *Searching for ambergris*.

You've heard the adage, "Give a man a fish and he'll eat for a day. But teach him to fish and he'll eat for a lifetime." Whale hunting revolutionizes the fishing industry! Whale hunting is not

about besting your competitors. That is a limited goal that will produce, at best, a consistent incremental advantage in your market. It
will never produce rapid growth.

Whale hunting changes the game. It focuses your attention on
growth that surpasses your competition to the point at which they
are no longer computed in your business equations.

Create Your Target Filter

Once you have determined your unique competitive advantage,
you are ready to define the characteristics of your ideal whale. You do
this by creating a target filter, a matrix of criteria to help you select
prospects. The goal of the target filter is to *exclude* most of the
whales in the oceans—to help you say *no*. The target filter helps
you evaluate new opportunities that come to you as well as to
choose those that you will actively hunt.

We imagine how the Inuit developed their target filter as they
planned for the upcoming hunt. They knew that whales swim at
different speeds: the orca whale (up to 30 mph) as opposed to the
beluga whale (2 to 6 mph). Whales come in different sizes: the blue
whale (up to 174 tons), as opposed to the orca (8,000 to 12,000
pounds). Based on previous hunting experience, they would
decide which of these characteristics they most valued. They knew
what would be their first, second, or third choices, if circumstances
of the whale hunt permitted them the choice. We assume that the
ideal whale would be a large, slow-moving animal, swimming close
to shore and that would float after its death. We know that they
sought a whale that was partially trapped among the ice floes. How
does this target filter work for a modern business?

You can follow this process as you conduct your own sales
review. Review and renew your portrait of the ideal buyer each year.

Convene your team to talk about the characteristics of your best buyers, those with whom you have had the most successful relationships for your company and theirs. What are their key characteristics? What made them ideal? Write down 10 to 20 different characteristics for your target buyer, your whale.

Here's an extended example from a professional services firm. The first time they engaged in this exercise, their target filter criteria, and their reason for choosing each one, looked like this:

- *Revenue:* This is a measure of size. They want a company big enough to benefit from their service but not at a size beyond where their services will be strategic.
- *Services:* They want a company that will have a need for comprehensive services.
- *Success history:* They want a growing company with a history of success.
- *Leadership:* They look for strong CEOs with a commitment to growth.
- *Market offering:* They want a company that offers a complex sale to their market.
- *Change events:* They want a company that is hungry to grow fast.
- *Organizational alignment:* They want a well-managed, functional company.
- *Referral:* They want a company to which one of their current clients has referred them.
- *Sales structure:* They want a company with a defined sales force and sales process.

When you have a good list of criteria that you think will be important, begin to add the metrics of the best descriptor in that category and the worst you might consider. Table 3.2 gives an example of this company's list, with the metrics that define an A target (most desirable) and a C target (least desirable).

Table 3.2	Initial Target Filter Criteria		
Filter Category	**A**	**B**	**C**
Revenue	$10M–$100M		<$10M
Fee opportunity	$250K+		<$50k
Services	Comprehensive Two-year+ relationship		Assessment only Discrete services only
Success history	Profitable Sustained Functioning culture		Turnaround Start-up Failing firms
Leadership	CEO VP of sales Extended team		No team
Market offering	Complex sale Business to business		Transaction Little consultation Procurement-based purchases
Limiters and change events	Appetite for change Defined events of change		Incremental change expectation
Organizational alignment	Strategic planning process Broad communication		No strategic planning process Hierarchical communication
Source	Referral Membership organization		Cold call
Sales structure	Direct and defined		Retail

The A column defines a perfect whale for this professional services firm as one with annual revenues between $10 million and $100 million. It has the opportunity to earn more than $250,000 over an extended engagement of two years or more. The company is profitable and has a history of growth. In place are a CEO, a vice president of sales, and an extended management team. The company makes products or provides services to other businesses (rather than direct to consumers), and its sales are complex. It has an appetite for growth and aggressive revenue goals in place. Perhaps the owner is preparing for a sale or an initial public offering. Or perhaps the company has recently taken on new investors. This company regularly conducts strategic planning exercises; managers implement the plan effectively; and the goals are broadly communicated and well understood among the employees. A former or current customer has recommended the professional services firm to the CEO.

Now read the metrics in the C column to get a sense of all of the companies that are not good whales for the professional services firm. The nontargeted companies are smaller than $10 million in annual revenue, and the fee opportunity is less than $50,000. They are interested only in specific services, not a comprehensive package. They are start-ups or in turnaround mode. The management team is not in place. These companies' products or services are transactional, and they usually sell to a procurement agent. They expect to grow incrementally. They do not follow a strategic plan, and they communicate poorly. No referrals are available.

You have probably made several observations as you read these descriptions. One is that the example firm may not find any perfect A companies. Second, the characteristics of the C category are unlikely to exist all in the same company. Third, it may be difficult for the firm to learn what they want to know about each of these criteria. And fourth, some of these criteria may be more important than the others.

You are right on all counts. We address each of these issues as we implement the target filter. But for now, we are still in the design phase. So let's move ahead in completing the design of the target filter.

The next step is to complete the target filter by filling in the metrics for your B-level target. Some of our clients define four categories, A through D, with finer distinctions between a B and a C. You will learn as you define your own target filter whether it is helpful to have another column. In the case we are describing, three categories were sufficient. Table 3.3 itemizes the next cut of the initial target filter.

Notice one surprise in the B column—the company's annual revenues. The ideal A target is a company whose revenue is between $10 million and $100 million. A company with greater than $100 million is a B to them, while a company with less than $10 million is a C. Bigger is not necessarily better.

Refine and Calibrate the Target Filter

Over time, the professional services firm added new criteria, as they learned from experience and as they continued to diversify their products and services. For example, they learned that they are most successful in selling to a company with prior experience in hiring external consultants, so they added that criterion to the target filter. They also redefined the size and shape of their whales to fit the greater diversity of products they now sell. The point is, the target filter is a living document that grows with the company and benefits from its market experience.

Table 3.3 Secondary Target Filter Criteria

Filter Category	A	B	C
Revenue	$10M–$100M	$100M+	<$10M
Fee opportunity	$250K+	$100K–$250K	<$50K
Services	Comprehensive Two-year+ relationship	Components only	Assessment training
Success history	Profitable Sustained Functioning culture	Declining market Variable profit history	Turnaround Start-up Failing firms
Leadership	CEO VP of sales Extended team	CEO Management team	No team
Market offering	Complex sale Business to business	Channel delivery Tight buying circle	Transaction Little consultation Procurement-based purchases
Limiters and change events	Appetite for change Defined events of change	Uncertainty	Incremental change expectation
Organizational alignment	Strategic planning process Broad communication	Tightly held strategy Tactical and function-based communication	No strategic planning process Tiered communication
Source	Referral Membership organization	Attendee at trade show	Cold call
Sales structure	Direct and defined	Two-step	Retail

One more refinement that you can make to your target filter is to weight certain categories in importance. As the target filter in Table 3.4 illustrates, the sample firm determined that three of their criteria are twice as important as each of the others: the target company's revenue, its market offering, and the source of its referral. They added a Weight column to capture this distinction.

Before we move on to applying the target filter to a universe of whales, let's look at a completely different target filter. Our point is that the target filter criteria are unique to your company. They are derived from your brand promise—that is, your company's unique value in the marketplace, and the characteristics of companies most likely to buy that particular unique value.

Our client, Langham Logistics, Inc., is a global freight management company that provides time-critical transportation of cargo as well as warehousing and distribution services. In a classic example of growth at the demand of its clients, Langham demonstrated its ability to handle complex transportation problems regardless of mode or geography. However, Langham needed to meet aggressive growth and profitability goals. Fewer than 20 major accounts, from a base of 200 customers, drove the company's revenue. Langham needed to understand how to pursue more large account sales. With help from The Whale Hunters, Langham defined and focused on the ideal prospect, one that would generate 10 times the annual run rate of its current average. Table 3.5 is the initial target filter it designed.

Through the process that we have described previously, we helped Langham to define its best prospect as a company with total revenues of greater than $500 million that has come to them through a personal referral. Its best prospects have 100 or more employees, use a full suite of services, and make 50 or more shipments

Table 3.4 Adding Weight Criterion to Target Filter

Filter Category	Weight	A	B	C
Revenue	2×	$10M–$100M	$100M+	<$10M
Fee opportunity		$250K+	$100K–$250K	<$50K
Services		Two-year+ relationship	Components only	Assessment training
Success history		Profitable Sustained Functioning culture	Declining market Variable profit history	Turnaround Start-up Failing firms
Leadership		CEO VP of sales Extended team	CEO Management team	No team
Market offering	2×	Complex sale Business to business	Channel delivery Tight buying circle	Transaction Little consultation Procurement-based purchases
Limiters and change events		Appetite for change Defined events of change	Uncertainty	Incremental change expectation
Organizational alignment		Strategic planning process Broad communication Shared history of all parties	Tightly held strategy Tactical and function-based communication	No strategic planning process Tiered communication
Source	2×	Referral Membership organization	Attendee at trade show	Cold call
Sales structure		Direct and defined	Two-step	Retail

Table 3.5 Sample Target Filter for Langham Logistics

Filter Category	A Opportunities	B Opportunities	C Opportunities	D Opportunities
Total revenue	$500M+	$50–$500M	$20–$50M	<$20M
Services revenue	$10M+	$1.0M–$10M	$100K–$1.0M	<$100K
Services used	Full suite	International and domestic	Domestic only	Specialty needed
Industry	Food and beverage	Electronic components	Furniture	Hazardous materials
Decision-maker source	Personal referral	Client referral	Six degrees of referral, RFQ/RFP	Cold source list
Number of employees	100+	40–100	10–40	<10
Volume of transactions	50+ shipments/ month	10–50 shipments/ month	5–10 shipments/ month	<5 shipments / month
Size of shipments	$1000+	$500–$1000	$100–$500	Less than $100
Number of locations	10+	5–10	2–5	1

a month, with a value of at least $1,000 each. Its whale also has 10 or more locations. Conversely, Langham will no longer waste time and personnel cold calling on any of the companies in the D column, which ship fewer than five shipments a month and have only one location.

In its first year of whale hunting, Langham doubled its number of key accounts by adding 16 new whale-sized customers. In the second year, it added an additional 24 whales. Revenue grew by 15 percent in the first year and 30 percent in the second year. Profitability has increased by 100 percent year over year.

Seldom will you find a prospective customer that rates an A in every category. You are looking for a preponderance of those A ratings that are most highly associated with the unique competitive advantage that you intend to solidify in your market. After you've drafted a target filter, test it against some of your current customers and prospects. You need to validate whether it helps you to discriminate, to filter out less desirable prospects and to rate highly those best suited to buy your services. First assign a numerical value to each of your columns—3 for an A score, 2 for a B score, and so on. Assign this customer a score for each criterion. If it's a weighted criterion, multiply the score by the weight. Then add all of the weighted scores for a target filter score. Table 3.6 gives an example of applying the target filter to a specific company. We've highlighted the score that has been assigned in each filter category.

In the target filter in Table 3.6, the maximum score for any single prospect would be 48 points—a score of 3 on each criterion, with four of the criteria weighted times 2. Obviously, a target filter score of 44 is extremely high. In this example from our client's history, the target filter score proved to be an excellent predictor of their success with this prospect, which later became a customer.

As you work through your target filter, don't hesitate to test, refine, and retest, until it begins to produce the results that you want.

In summary, *know the whale*, phase one of the Whale Hunters' Process, is an extended discovery process in which you explore your unique advantages in the marketplace, refine your sales offer, and define key characteristics of the whales that you want to attract.

Table 3.6 Applying Target Filter

Customer: ABC Corporation

Filter Category	Weight	Score	Weighted	A = 3	B = 2	C = 1
Revenue	2×	3	6	$10M–$100M	$100M+	<$10M
Fee opportunity		3	3	$250K+	$100K–$250K	<$50K
Services		2	2	Strategic Visioning Culture Change Two-year+ relationship	Sales change Process mapping One- to three-year vision	Assessment training Tracking
Success history		2	2	Profitable Sustained Functioning culture	Declining Market Variable profit history	Turnaround Start-up Failing firms
Leadership		3	3	CEO VP of sales Extended team	CEO Management team	No team
Market offering	2×	3	6	Complex sale Business to Business	Channel delivery Tight buying circle	Transaction Little consultation Procurement-based purchases

(Continued)

Table 3.6 (*Continued*)

Customer: ABC Corporation

Filter Category	Weight	Score	Weighted	A = 3	B = 2	C = 1
Limiters and change events		3	3	Appetite for change Defined events of change	Uncertainty	Incremental change expectation
Organizational alignment		1	1	Strategic planning process Broad communication Shared history of all parties	Tightly held strategy Tactical and function-based communication	No strategic planning process Tiered communication
Source	2×	3	6	Referral Membership organization	Attendee at session	Cold call
Ownership	2×	3	6	Private, closely held	Private, broadly held	Public
Sales structure		2	2	Direct and defined	Two-step	Retail
Target filter score			44			

Once you know what your whales look like and how they behave, the next steps are to determine who they are, where they are, and how many you want to track. Those are the skills of *seek the whale*, coming up in the next chapter.

Know the Whale Action Items

- *Define the ocean in which your whales swim.*
- *Chart the waters to understand your position versus your competitors.*
- *Create a target filter that will identify only 4 percent of the whales in your ocean.*
- *Test your target filter against current whale accounts, and revise as needed.*

Please visit www.thewhalehunters.com to download the sales process tools introduced in this chapter.

4

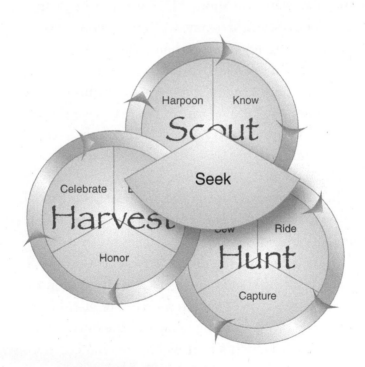

Send Out the Scouts

WHALES CAN BE DIFFICULT TO SPOT.

That defies logic. Whales dwarf every other animal in their world. Their hearts are the size of a Volkswagen. Ask anyone who has seen a breaching humpback and you will hear the description of an awe-inspiring event. Presumably, whales would be hard to miss.

Nevertheless, as ancient village scouts scoured the horizon, seeking signs of approaching whales, the creatures could slip by undetected. Sliding up the chilly western coastline of North America, coming from their traditional winter homes in today's Baja, California, the whales blended well into their environment. Even though spring was commencing as they made their journey north, the days were still short. Skies were overcast much of the day. Young scouts scanned a gray horizon—a gray ocean meeting a gray sky—searching for a gray whale. Often, a whale passed for a rock, a shadow, a mass of debris. So, despite months of village preparation, the huge mammals could move by undetected.

Will another whale come within range to save the village from a long year of hard work and hunger? Will another year of fighting to meet the minimal needs of the group prevent progress and growth? There are no promises. Every opportunity is crucial.

Yet when scouts miss the signs of an approaching whale, catching sight only of a huge fluke far to the north heading for a summer home, cool heads must prevail. A wild rush to catch a whale that has slipped by into the distance is almost always a mistake. Launching a hunting boat is a dangerous and costly endeavor. Valuable team members and scarce resources are at risk. The reputation and morale of the hunting team and the entire village are on the line. You only launch a boat when the chances are high for a successful hunt.

The balance is delicate.

Responsibility for this vital scouting task is primarily in the hands of two types of villagers: the scouts and the shaman.

The scouts, usually boys between the ages of seven and twelve, have been taught to closely investigate the horizon, watching for signs of approaching whales.

In the best cases, they see the evidence of approaching whales well before the big animals arrive. They look for signs of flocks of birds and smaller sea predators like dolphins that follow the same schools of small fish and krill that feed the huge whales. A successful scout gives advance warning of the approach of the whales to the village and its shaman so that they can launch a hunting boat deliberately.

Scouts are intelligence gatherers. They are the community's eyes and ears. With the right information, the village is able to maximize the harvest. With the wrong information, the next winter will be long and difficult.

The shaman occupies a higher position in the village hierarchy. He or she is a holy person, a go-between to the physical and the spiritual worlds. The shaman weighs the information brought in by the scouts, considers the village's preparedness, consults the signs in the environment, and only then decides whether to launch a hunting boat.

Your Scouting Plan

With the Whale Hunters' Process, growing businesses learn to use this proven, deliberate system to find and capture whale-sized prospects. This process enables your business to maximize sales by bringing knowledge, deliberation, and focus to the sales process. It helps you identify the customers you want, naturally culling out the whales that would waste time and resources, allowing your team of hunters the best possible chance of bringing in a new whale-sized customer or client. It also helps you focus your sales approach—by providing clear maps and charts to follow for a successful hunt that you can replicate time after time.

You have identified your *unique competitive advantage*, or what you have to sell. Using a target filter, you have isolated the characteristics that would indicate a whale company that is most likely to respond to the value you bring.

Now it is time to determine which whales to hunt and when is the optimal season to pursue each of them. The key whale hunting tools in this phase are:

- Shaman selection
- Scouting plan (a map of how you will research and track your whales)
- Whale chart (a list of the whales you may hunt)
- Dossier template (a format for scouts to use in reporting information
- Whale signs (a timeline of the market and buying trends of your whale)

Select a Shaman

Selecting the right shaman is key to assuring the future of your company as you try to develop a whale hunting mentality within your work force. The shaman frequently comes out of sales, although the position is much broader than the traditional sales or sales management role. The shaman is responsible for the development and implementation of the Whale Hunters' Process throughout the village. It is up to the shaman to infuse the energy and rigor needed to keep the village focused and on track to complete the whale hunt. The shaman is instrumental in changing the company culture to embrace the whale hunting mentality, and must be a part of the strategy team from the beginning. If you are instituting whale hunting for the first time, select your shaman as the first team member.

Sometimes this person already holds the position of sales manager. In larger companies, the shaman might be a sales vice president. In smaller and midsize companies, the CEO may be the de facto shaman. If you are that shaman/chief, be certain that you have the requisite skills to fulfill both roles: you should be strong, with proven management skills, capable of embracing change. Introducing the new concept of whale hunting to the harpooners and to the rest of the village will be part of your responsibility. This whale hunt metaphor is new to everyone. The terms and language are new, and the basic premise of focusing on a small group of prospective customers is counterintuitive to what your team has been taught or has experienced. If you are your company's harpooner, and you don't report to a shaman, you can help to educate yourself and the management team about the importance of this function.

Maybe you are a member of the key executive team that will make joint decisions about which whales to hunt. At this point, the title does not matter, but the roles make the difference between a hunt supported by the entire village and a merely random kill. The village needs to decide systematically which whales to consider hunting. The decision of which whales to hunt is not a random or sporadic one. It is not made opportunistically by a single individual; rather it is made based on the studied wisdom of the village. So, in the following discussion, think of the shaman as the person or team responsible for allocating the village's resources to undertake a dangerous and expensive hunt.

The shaman orchestrates the work of different types of people who are filling very different roles. Supervising the ambitious, creative people who are the harpooners in the whale-hunting process is particularly challenging. Harpooners—and you may be one of them—are often successful salespeople in more traditional systems. They do not enjoy being supervised. They are often the sales "magicians" who have brought in lucrative deals in the past by working alone. They trust their own instincts and may find working in a team environment difficult. A good shaman must turn these lone hunters into members of the team, who understand the process and appreciate and even depend on the input of the other crew members in the whale boat.

It is important for the shaman to repeat and reinforce the metaphor, language, and concepts of the whale hunt, especially in the early stages of the process. The shaman should insist that the language of the whale hunt be used. Using the hunting terms for each step, as the company goes through the process, helps everyone understand the importance of each move. It also brings a contagious excitement to the process. Call the shaman the shaman, the harpooner the harpooner, and the whale chart the whale chart. Allow your team to visualize how they are using a system that has been effective for centuries.

Understand that it will be necessary, as you move from one of the nine whale hunting phases to the next, to review the system to show the village how each step fits into the overall plan. It does require a leap of faith for the village to accept all of these new and different concepts. The shaman looks for ways to encourage and reward success and to celebrate each advance from one phase to the next, to ensure that the system becomes part of your company's culture.

Identify the Scouts

Now it's time for an important decision: Who will perform the scouting functions? While some of our clients use sophisticated research tools and have staff members who conduct market research, others have little or no experience in formal market research. We'll assume that you are the shaman, chief, or harpooner in your organization and that you probably do not have the skills, interests, time, or talents required to be an effective scout. The scout's job is to keep the shaman and the harpooners informed at all times about the marketplace of whales that are of interest to the company.

You may have a researcher on your marketing or business development team who will take over the scouting role. College interns serve as good additions to a scouting team. Part-time scouts may do double-duty by fulfilling other administrative positions.

If you are a harpooner, we can almost guarantee that you will not be a good scout. In fact, if you are an independent salesperson, hire someone to fulfill the scouting role for you. Scouts look like polar opposites of the harpooners. On a personality test or a preferred activities inventory, scouts and harpooners occupy extreme ends of the spectrum. The person who fills the scout role is seldom interested in sales as a profession. Likewise, the type of detailed research that scouting requires can be boring and distracting to the best salespeople. Find someone within your organization or bring in someone capable of doing this task and enjoying it.

The best scouts are unusually adept at pattern recognition. Scouts are detail oriented. They should be curious, with good memories for even the most insignificant deviation from the norm. They are patient and capable of following and understanding trends.

However, the importance of the scout position goes well beyond the status of the person filling it. A truly creative and committed scout adds significant value to the whale-hunting process. Like the Inuit who travel to the shoreline each morning to scan the waves for a large flock of birds or a few dolphins, your scouts are looking for something out of the ordinary. They are looking for a change, a sign that can help you anticipate a business change.

Your scouting plan needs to include the initial research that the scouts will accomplish to populate your whale chart. It will include the templates that you prefer for dossiers on key whale prospects, both the initial scouting dossier and the more elaborate hunting dossier. You will identify key whale signs as part of the scouting plan, and you will design a mechanism for the scouts to report to the shaman and the harpooners what they are learning about the activities of the whales whose behavior they are observing.

Old leadership skills necessary for putting each player on your team into the right position come into play here. Don't make the scout selection lightly.

Create Your Whale Chart

The target filter directs your efforts to identify specific whales that you may decide to hunt. Before you apply your target filter to the entire marketplace, run a calibration exercise using your current customers. Does your target filter identify your current best customers? Will it help to weed out those current customers that are less than ideal—for example, too small, too problematic, too difficult or demanding, slow to pay? If you aren't yet doing business with whales, you can move directly to the next step. But if you have or have had some very large customers and accounts, do a test drive with the target filter.

Once you are satisfied with your target filter, you can begin to create your whale chart. The whale chart is an inventory of the ideal whales caught in your target filter. Moving from the target filter to the whale chart takes you from the abstract profile of a perfect customer to a concrete list of companies, by name, that meet your criteria. First, you conduct a research project to find those prospects. If you have identified your scout or scouting team, this is where they begin their work.

We'll start at the beginning of a whale chart research project. The task is to survey the marketplace to find companies that match, or come close to matching, the various target filter criteria. Here's how to counsel your scout:

1. *Use the library*. Your public library, college or university library, and local or state chamber of commerce research departments can introduce you to free or low-cost databases for business searches. Librarians can also help you to identify and evaluate data sources that you might want to purchase.
   - Some obvious business data sources are Dun & Bradstreet, Hoover, and LexisNexis. Look at an NAICS code chart to search within specific industries.
   - ReferenceUSA is a business data source to which libraries buy a subscription, making much of the database available to patrons at no cost.
   - A very powerful database for which you would pay a subscription price is TheListInc.com. Providing names of key

executives and continually updating data comprise key selling points for this service.

- Within your own industry, membership associations and trade journals provide research directions specific to your needs or offer publications with detailed market research.

2. *Select relevant databases and search them for companies matching some of your core criteria.* Some criteria can be determined only after an initial phone call or visit, so focus on the ones that are most readily available. These include annual sales, numbers of employees, industry classification, geographic locations, and executive names and biographies.

3. *Create a list of companies that meet your criteria.* Make your list in the form of a table or spreadsheet where you can record contact information and enter the key criteria related to industry, size, revenue, geography, and so on. Then score them against your weighted criteria. How many companies do you want on your whale chart? In part, that is a function of your size and your sales resources—1,000 companies are probably too many; 10 companies are too few. Since your scout will need to complete detailed research on each of the companies listed on the whale chart, somewhere between 25 and 100 probably optimizes your initial search. If you have multiple products across multiple markets, you may prefer a whale chart for each of your key markets.

A whale chart is nothing more than a list, and how you manage it depends on your process for managing other sales data. It can be as simple as a table or spreadsheet, or it can be integrated into an elaborate sales or enterprise management database. The choice is yours.

Example Whale Chart Search Results

We searched LexisNexis.com for a list of commercial printers with less than $100 million in annual revenues and fewer than 2,500 employees. The search yielded 93 companies in the United States and Canada that meet those criteria.

We searched for commercial printers with annual revenues between $1 and $2 billion, and got nine hits. Ninety-three companies would make a good whale chart. Nine companies are not enough. You would need to modify your annual revenue criteria or expand the geography internationally in order to generate a larger list. But those nine companies may be at the top of your expanded list!

Once your scout has produced a whale chart, it is time to learn more about those whales. The shaman oversees and stays closely involved in this process. It is the shaman's responsibility to decide which whales the village will hunt and, ultimately, to decide when the time is right to launch a boat after a particular whale.

The next step in this responsibility requires learning a lot more about the particular whales that you may choose to hunt.

Create Dossiers

After completing the whale chart, the shaman begins the work of narrowing down the list to the very best prospects. Assign the scouts to an initial round of reconnaissance based on the whale chart. The next step in the scouting process is to develop a basic report, or *dossier*, on each company in your whale chart. We call this report a *scouting dossier*. Scouts can obtain information through many intelligence vendors, including those used to populate the whale chart.

If your prospects are public companies, you will find ample disclosure on their Web sites, especially through a close reading and study of the company's annual report. To research private companies, scouts will need to dig deeper, calling the company to request annual reports and combing secondary sources. If your scout calls a prospective whale, instruct him or her to be direct and honest in the request for information. "Hello," the scout may say to the person who answers the incoming call on the switchboard. "I am Gina Fontenot from XYZ Company. We are interested in learning how to do business with your company. Will you send me a copy of your annual report? Can you tell me the name of the person who is responsible for buying——for your company? Will you give me his or her contact information? Thank you very much." If the first person the scout speaks to is unwilling or unable to provide information, the scout should request to be connected to someone else who is responsible for purchasing the products or services that you sell. Keep in mind that this is not a sales call in any form. It is simply a request for information. If the whale is reluctant to provide rudimentary information to the marketplace, that response should become part of your dossier.

Table 4.1 is an example of an initial scouting dossier for a company that is listed on your whale chart.

Prepare the Hunting Dossier

Armed with the initial dossiers for all companies on your whale chart, the leadership team should convene to determine which of the whales seem to warrant further research and consideration. Test them against your target filter to select the top 25 or 50 or 100, depending upon your own size and capacity to hunt. This selection

Table 4.1 Example Scouting Dossier*

Company name	Newco Technologies
Address	123 Grand Vista Road
City, state, zip	Valley View, CA 94000
Main phone	(408) 123-4567
URL	www.newco.com
Ticker symbol	NEWCO
Sector	Computer software
Description	The company makes software to optimize the performance of enterprise systems. It is a business-to-business provider that targets its sales to senior IT executives. It also offers training and consulting services, as well as selling software.
Key products	Business technology optimization products, consulting, training, and maintenance
Major customers	Cingular, Wal-Mart, Dell
Market position	Third in North American market
Key competitors	BMS Software, OptiWare
Industry/equity analysts	John Hickman, Goldman Sachs; Cheryl David, Morgan Stanley; Oliver Ornstein, JP Morgan
Fiscal Year-End	December
Our competitors	Unknown at this point
History with us	No prior history with this company
Messaging/areas of opportunity	Marketing materials and Web site do not reflect the quality of the service they want to portray

(Continued)

Table 4.1 *(Continued)*			
Company name	**Newco Technologies**		
Financial data	Year 1	Year 2	Year 3
Revenue	685.5	506.5	400.1
Gross margin	85.8%	88.2%	88.7%
Operating margin	14.1%	16%	16.8%
EPS	.83	.45	.74
Assets	$2,020		
Debt	$1,439		
Equity	581		

*Data contrived for this example.

process is both art and science. If people on your team have information to suggest that a particular whale is a good prospect, or not a good prospect, listen to their advice.

When you have narrowed the initial whale chart, return the edited list to the scout and request a much more detailed dossier on each of the remaining whales. Now the scout should supplement basic information through independent sources, such as analysts' reports, industry studies, and news. Collect relevant information that each company has released through their Web sites, annual reports, white papers or press releases. For public companies, scouts often participate in conference calls or webinars with the chief executive, in which the company is explaining its financial situation and future prospects to the market.

The importance of the dossier material cannot be overemphasized. The dossier takes the form of a paper or electronic folder or file profiling the prospect. For instance, if the whale operates through a number of important locations around the country, the dossier should list the addresses and contact information of each location. It also identifies important decision makers within the company, financial history, ties with other vendors and suppliers, business partnerships, and alliances. The hunting dossiers should also include news clippings from trade and business press—even pictures, graphs and charts, and videos or CDs of television coverage. Although you are trying to obtain information on your whale before it becomes popularly known, you must still stay aware of the widely circulated information. Revealing your ignorance of commonly known information about a prospect can be dangerous.

Search for information about senior executives and board members. Learn who they are, what they respect, and what ambitions they hold for their company. Understand how Wall Street estimates the company. Most important, look for connections between your company and your whale target. Following are some examples of informational fields that might be added to the hunting dossier.

Contacts

Identify key members of the management team and board of directors. Google the officers' names to discover boards on which they serve and organizations of which they are members. Then look for possible connections between people you know and people affiliated with the whale company. Think of this scouting practice as "six degrees of separation." The purpose is to find an introduction into

Table 4.2 Contact Information in the Dossier

First Name	Last Name	Title	Our Relationship
Thomas	Ringo	CEO	None known
Lawrence	Weatherford	SVP, Sales	Used to work for Althus when Bill Roberts was in sales there; a possible entry point
Julio	Gonzalez	CFO	None known
Frances	Allen	COO	Member of Women in Business chapter; look for relationship through Marilyn Carter

the company. Consider joining one or more of the many business networking sites in the Internet, such as Linked In or Networking for Professionals. Record information in the dossier, whether in print or digital format (see Table 4.2, for an example).

Digital or Print Portfolio

The expanded dossier should include industry reports, Web documents, press releases, new product offerings, earnings predictions, and so forth. The emphasis is on finding evidence of change, especially impending change, which can be a signal for opportunity.

Once the initial hunting dossier is complete, scouts and the shaman will develop a set of criteria for whale signs, and scouts will watch for these signs systematically.

Watch for Whale Signs

Each day scouts carefully amass more intelligence that can be taken to the shaman. Like the Inuit scouts who watch for the approach of

birds and small fish that precede the whales, your scouts are searching for whale signs. These signs come in a variety of forms, but
generally they are bits of industry or business intelligence that
can signal a selling opportunity for you at the whale-sized prospect
company. It is up to you to define for your scouts what constitutes
whale signs—indicators of readiness to buy.

In some industries, mergers and acquisitions are whale signs. If
one of your prospects is bought by or buys another company, that
can be a clear sign that it might be time to mount a full-scale effort
to sell your product or service to that prospect. For instance, when
the merged companies attempt to make their computer systems
compatible, they may need new technology. They may require office
space, architectural or engineering design, moving and storage services, human resources counsel, strategic planning and business
development advice, financial services, printing, marketing, communications systems, Web site redesign, and so on, through a very
long list of products and services. At the same time, the current vendors to each company, regardless of the service they provide, may be
required to enter into a bidding process for continued work with the
newly merged company, thus opening the doors to new providers.

In addition, key executives who have either championed your
company or, conversely, looked unfavorably on your efforts in the
past may be shuffled around. The friendly executive's new company
might make a good addition to your list of whale prospects. And
the loss of the problem executive might open the door for a new
approach to the original prospect.

As the scouts go about their work of keeping current their
detailed dossiers on each whale prospect, these whale signs will
reveal themselves. The scouts must be well trained to the point
that the whale signs quickly catch their attention. Then they must

be good communicators, sensing when and how to report to the shaman the changes they have spotted. They must also know that the shaman will listen to them and express confidence in their research skills and the judgment they will develop over time.

This free communication also extends to the harpooners, who can relay bits of industry gossip and news to the scouts. The scouts are then in a position to take that otherwise worthless information and put it together with the scout research that they do daily, to reveal an important whale sign.

This information collection continues through the entire whale hunting process. In fact, the whale dossiers are evolving documents; they are never complete. Even when a company drops in priority, or is not being hunted for one reason or another, the dossier stays current.

Scouts are constantly updating the relevant information, on a set schedule, by going back to the old intelligence sources and to new sources they locate along the way.

Define Whale Signs

Whale signs are signals gleaned in advance of the "easy indicators" to reveal when a large prospect is ready to hear your message. The importance of the continuous scouting process is that it lets you see the signs of the approaching whale before your competitors spot them. Take, for instance, our example of the personnel change. If you find out about the change from the local business publication or newspaper business page, you are probably too late. Your competitors are scouring that information as closely as you are. The important intelligence needs to come to you through your research of the whale signs. You won't completely stop your existing system of sales networking and researching the common industry publications. However, you will find yourself relying on them less and less as you see the whale signs before they reveal themselves through the old and easy sources.

For example, a commercial real estate company might identify layoffs by companies in its target area as a whale sign. After a layoff, the real estate company might go in and take the resulting excess office space, subletting it, and leasing back a smaller space to the former tenant. The real estate firm would benefit from both sides of the transaction.

The real estate firm's second indicator might be a company's growth rate that is greater than 12 percent. History and experience revealed during the knowing the whale process that if a company is growing at more than 12 percent, it does now or will soon need to expand its office space.

Using the Whale Hunters' Process, this real estate company sees that it needs to identify firms that are preparing for major layoffs or are growing at greater than 12 percent before these facts are commonly recognized in the marketplace. It needs to spot these changes before the growing or receding company actually puts out a request for qualifications (RFQ) saying it needs a change of office space. The real estate company needs to know before the intelligence becomes commoditized.

Your company cannot watch for whale signs if you are scanning the entire ocean. You have to narrow your attention to only those whales that have been caught in your target filter. A properly run system of searching for whale signs can uncover this information before it becomes common knowledge. In this case, for instance, the scout can be doing a monthly or weekly search of the D&B ratings of the whales on the whale chart. If there is a ratings change, the shaman can be tipped off and more research can be done to see if this is a whale sign that should prompt the launching of a boat. Whale signs should have the following characteristics:

- Predictive of upcoming changes that may create opportunity
- Precede more obvious market signs (signs all competitors are watching)
- Can be identified and market-monitored by scouts
- Factual, not emotional or interpretive
- Signify opportunity: timing, scope, and/or location

Table 4.3 lists a number of potential whale signs.

Table 4.3 Example Whale Signs

Indicator	Event	Source	Frequency
Analyst	Downgrade	Web data	Auto-notify
Key personnel change	Change	Press release	Watch
Market share	Downgrade	Subscription service	Quarterly
Competitor M & A	Purchase	Yahoo	Auto-notify
Missed earnings	Missed projection	Yahoo	Auto-notify
Stock price	Downgrade	Yahoo	Auto-notify
Agency of record	Change	Yahoo	Auto-notify
Capital structure	Change	Web data	Auto-notify
Technology	Patent, enterprise system, alliance	Trades, web data	Watch
D&B Rating	Change	Web data	Auto-notify

Note that scouts can set auto-alerts from Yahoo or Google. They can subscribe to Really Simple Syndication (RSS) feeds from the company's Web site or blog, as well as subscribe to RSS feeds from industry news sources, both professional and anecdotal.

Our client, SGI, Inc., is a logistics and fulfillment expert that handles marketing materials for their customers. As an exceptionally process-oriented company, they have been very effective in implementing the Whale Hunters' Process. After embarking on the whale hunting path, SGI hired a new person to serve in the role of scout. This person fulfills a pivotal role, which encompasses both scout and harpooner (which will be detailed in the next chapter). Not only does she conduct research on the whale prospects and prepare dossiers, she also "opens the door" into the whale, conducting the initial exploratory meetings and organizing the initial meeting between representatives of SGI and the whale.

The final piece of work to implement in your scouting process is for the shaman to define explicitly the expectations for the scouts' performance. What is the time frame for creating the initial dossiers? How frequently should the scouts update each dossier? How and how often should the scout communicate this information to the shaman? We advocate that you expect the scout to seek out actively information from the harpooners and the shaman, to manage the scouting process in all its phases, and to report regularly on progress.

Now that you have selected your shaman, populated your whale chart, completed dossiers, and set up your system for tracking whale signs, you are ready to hunt. The next steps are to get close to your targeted whales in order to set the harpoon. These methods are outlined in the next chapter.

Send Out the Scouts Action Items

- *Identify the shaman who will manage your whale hunting system.*
- *Select and train scouts and provide resources to learn about your targeted whales.*
- *Populate your whale chart with the names of less than 4 percent of your market.*
- *Complete initial dossiers and implement communication plans among scouts, shaman, and harpooners.*
- *Define whale signs and implement a tracking system.*
- *Create metrics for scouts' performance expectations.*

Please visit www.thewhalehunters.com to download the sales process tools introduced in this chapter.

5

Set the Harpoon

WHEN THE SCOUTS REPORTED seeing whale signs and the shaman blessed the hunt, the harpooner sprang into action in a leadership role. The Inuit harpooner earned that distinction by virtue of having been successful in previous hunts. Typically, the harpooner's family owned the umiak that would be launched to hunt a whale. They would also have been gifted and diligent in creating the harpooning tools—a sharp object that could pierce the whale's blubber, a strong rope that could withstand the stress of the upcoming ride, and various weights and bladders that would slow the whale's progress.

The harpooner was in charge of the umiak—standing or sitting in the bow, directing the boat's course, bearing the ultimate responsibility for bringing the boat alongside a whale. Under the harpooner's direction, the crew would set out from the edge of ice in the direction where they believed the whales would be arriving. They had prepared to be on the water for weeks, not knowing how long it would take them to find the whales, get close to a whale, sink the harpoon, and, ultimately, bring the whale back to land.

The oarsmen paddled, and fulfilled other roles as well, such as fishing for food along the way and keeping the line free and untangled. The shaman oversaw all activities, while chanting to remind them of the rituals of the hunt, singing songs to calm the waters, and praying to bring the whales into sight.

They hoped to find a whale that swam between ice floes where they could maneuver it into a vulnerable position. If they were lucky, they could approach a whale that was resting on the surface of the water, although only half of the whale's brain sleeps at one time. But often their whale was in open waters, making the harpooner's job even more dangerous.

When they spotted a whale, the crew paddled the boat until they were alongside the whale, to enable the harpooner to set the harpoon. You may be imagining images of a whaler hurling a harpoon against a whale from a distance. But in reality, throw a harpoon and odds are it will bounce back. No, the harpooner had to be up close. Sometimes he left his umiak and jumped onto the back of the whale to set the harpoon.

The harpoon was attached to a long length of rope, managed by the oarsmen. Its purpose was to attach the whale to the umiak. The harpoon typically did not kill the whale; rather, it wounded it, thus annoying it and provoking it to action. The whale had several options. It might dive, waiting silently underwater for an hour or more, then catapulting to the surface, perhaps capsizing the boat. It could turn out to sea, hauling the little boat behind it. Or it could swim along the shoreline, hoping to rid itself of the pest. Whatever the whale's action, the whale hunters in the small umiak were in for a ride.

Reconnaissance

Harpooning is a core strategy for a fast-growth business. The time to launch a boat is when you have done everything possible to ensure a successful hunt. With a list of ideal whales in hand, your shaman uses the scouts to search for signs of whale movement. Timing matters; the shaman needs to make good decisions about which whales to hunt and when to go after them. Scouting helps you decide when a whale on your chart might be ready to hunt, as well as when to closely follow good prospects that for some reason are not candidates for a full-on hunt at this time—having recently signed with a competitive vendor in your space, for instance. The shaman uses the scouting information as the primary intelligence to decide when to launch a boat.

Scouting will reveal some prospects that seem ready for an approach, candidates for an immediate and all-out sales effort. The shaman will have organized the final list of the best whales into groups of prospects, and assigned each harpooner a group of prospects—five perhaps, or eight. Not a large number. Whale hunting is about landing fewer, bigger deals than you have done in the past. Depending on your company's size and resources, you may have one or more salespeople who will become whale hunters, as well as other salespeople who will continue to fish and to farm existing accounts. We are not suggesting that you make an immediate or abrupt move to whale hunting as your sole means of survival. It is an evolving process.

When all of the initial research is complete, and the shaman and other company leaders have determined which whales to hunt first, the harpooner's role becomes very important. In the Whale Hunters' Process, the harpooner is a salesperson who has been assigned to lead the hunt for certain whale-sized prospects. In a sales deal with a whale—a complex deal—the harpooner's role differs markedly from the traditionally defined sales role. Rather than behaving like rock star salespersons who find the lead, pitch the deal, close it, and bring it home, harpooners are the leaders of a cross-functional team, each member having a carefully defined role to play in securing the deal. Whale deals take longer, cost more, and present greater challenges than the average deal.

Because the process is so costly, the chief and the shaman, *not the harpooner*, should be the ones to decide when to pursue a new prospect. A failed hunt can be harmful and demoralizing, so someone who can identify when the company is financially ready and with the right personnel in place to launch a whale boat and to harvest the whale must control that decision.

Our client, Ontario Systems, is a developer of accounts receivable software. Because they must do an extensive installation after the sale, it is extremely important in their business to achieve a high level of consistency between the client's expectations, which are set during the sales process, and the product delivery, which may be completed a year or more after the deal is inked. We helped them to develop a custom flowchart map for each phase of their sales and implementation processes. The excerpt shown here illustrates the orchestration of the earliest steps in the sales process, in this case involving the customer, the harpooner, the marketing team representative, and the shaman.

The scout, the chief, and the village at large have no specific responsibilities during the reconnaissance steps. The shaman takes responsibility to monitor the progress of each whale account as it moves forward through this process.

The harpooner has three major responsibilities at this point:

- Get close to the whale.
- Get the whale's attention.
- Garner key information from the whale.

The harpooner's first contacts with the whale are designed to complete your company's dossier, answering key questions that your scouts could not determine from outside sources. The harpooner needs to find the appropriate point of entry, listen and learn, fill in the blanks, and begin to assess the opportunity. The initial meeting or two may be qualifying meetings on both sides, with you qualifying your prospect and the whale qualifying you. The harpooner will only be arranging meetings with a whale your company has made a commitment to hunt, should the harpooner find that the time seems to be right.

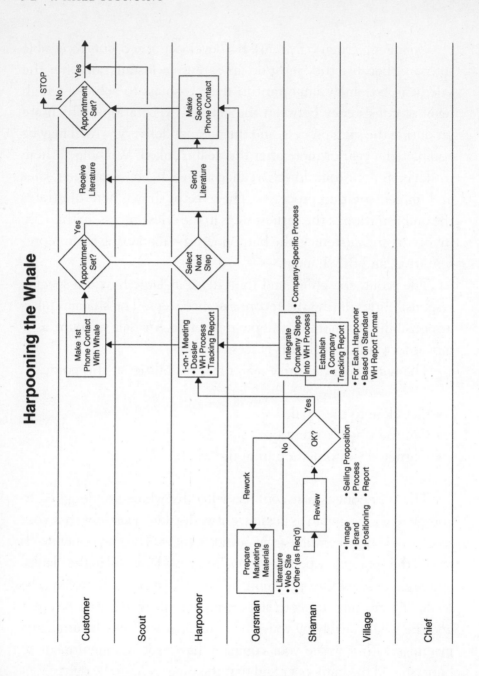

Harpooning the Whale

So before you even authorize a reconnaissance, company leadership should be satisfied that you can present yourself properly to a whale and can handle a whale if you land it. Both of these issues may require some investment in order to give the harpooner the tools, equipment, and crew that he or she will oversee.

Make Contact

Let's assume you are the harpooner. You have your assignment—get close to this whale. How will you go about it? First, you'll study the dossier and arm yourself with knowledge about the whale. Then, you'll put together the right tools for the job.

- Your sharp, pointed harpoon—a brief, specific, well-honed message
- Carefully selected, professionally prepared materials to support your message
- Key questions that you will ask the whale

The next step is to decide who you will contact and in what manner. The dossier and the scouting information should provide you with names, titles, and contact information for key executives. Your six-degrees-of-separation work may have revealed a current customer, friend of your company, or mutual acquaintance. Ask that person to make an introduction to the person you believe is the best initial contact. Then follow up with a phone call requesting an appointment.

Your first meeting sets the tone for the entire relationship to follow. As the representative of a smaller company, you must appear from the first moment—the introductory phone call and request for the meeting—to be suitably professional, confident, and knowledgeable.

Be certain that you know with whom you will be meeting and how many people will be present. Under no circumstances should you go alone on a sales call to a team of buyers. If they will have three people present, for example, you need two. If they're bringing five, take three. We'll have more to say about their buying team and your sales team later; but for now, the important principle is to know what to expect before you get close to the whale.

Control the Aperture of Perception

One key component of the sales process for a whale is what we call the *aperture of perception*. It's a photographic analogy. Simply stated, the person behind the camera deliberately selects the point of view, the scope of revelation, the interplay of background and foreground, the relative light and darkness. Just as there is artistry in setting up the photo shoot, there should be artistry in your presentation to the prospect.

Your prospects will see you through the aperture—the opening—that you create. Your success differential is to create the aperture by deliberation, not by default. It's up to you to select all of the details that your prospect experiences.

We are not suggesting that you misrepresent your business. Rather, we suggest that you purposefully present in the best possible light the high points of your people, your promises, your processes, and your production. This presentation calls for systematic preparation and implementation.

In early visits, you will rely on print and digital materials, as well as your own interpersonal qualities and image of professionalism. As the hunt continues, however, the buyers will get much closer to your entire village, so prepare to manage the perceptions throughout your company and to engage multiple employees in contributing to these perceptions. The top 10 elements of your aperture of perception are as follows.

1. *Image:* Is your website pertinent and professional?
2. *Voice:* Have you prepared every receptionist to handle and route calls from your prospect?
3. *Knowledge:* Does every member of your team demonstrate deep knowledge of the prospect's business?
4. *Quality:* Is your proposal or statement of work correct, attentive to detail, attractive, and stylistically appropriate?
5. *Depth:* Are you engaging your subject matter experts in specific ways to support the sales process?
6. *Commitment:* Can your prospect observe a commitment to excellent delivery in all interactions with your company?
7. *Enthusiasm:* Does your entire "village" express a desire to serve this customer?
8. *Respect:* Can you ensure that all of your company's deliverables to the prospect are completed on time?
9. *Courtesy:* Will everyone on your team go the extra mile in arranging for site visits, conference calls, team meetings, and other events?
10. *Sincerity:* Will your prospect feel a sincere desire for their business from every encounter with your team members?

The measure of success for each of these criteria is not whether it is good or bad, but whether it will distinguish your firm from other suppliers and, thus, garner respect from a much larger customer. You need to present with the same level of safety and security that will be apparent from your larger competitors. Don't launch until you are confident about how you will present yourself to the whale.

Ask Critical Questions

Your first visit does not involve making a sale. Rather, your mission is to learn whether pursuing this particular whale is a good idea for your company. Therefore, you have questions to ask and answers to process. Conduct an X-ray of the whale. Figure out the reporting structures, formal and informal. Try to get an understanding of the budget. Learn who currently provides the products or services that you would provide.

As you prepare questions, first determine what key pieces of information you need to know to decide whether you want the customer. Turn your good questions into great questions with thought and practice.

The best introductory questions help you to understand the whale's history. They predict future behavior and describe practice. They open the door to discussion, they promote reflection, and they allow you to understand whether the whale is willing to be vulnerable by telling you the truth.

For example, here is a list of key pertinent questions specific to the insurance industry. In each case, we've annotated what the harpooner would learn from the answers to these questions.

- Describe the process you used to select your current agent. What one change would you make to the process? Talk about the agent you did not select.
  Did they use a process that would be a good process for you? Are you more like the agent they selected or rejected? Do they have a clear process and are they able to improve upon it?
- Which services being currently provided do you find most beneficial?

Which services do they value? Which services do you have that they would probably deem beneficial?

- Describe any issues where your current provider is/was unable to fulfill your expectations.
  How satisfied are they with the incumbent? Can you fulfill expectations that the current provider cannot meet?
- What are the two last changes made to your loss control program that had the most impact?
  How well do they understand loss control? Will they be interested in new ideas from you?
- Tell us about the professional associations your management team belongs to. How active are you? What do you think is the impact on your business?
  What kind of people are they? What kind of company do they represent?
- What has driven your success in the area of safety and reduction in claims? What things are you doing differently now versus five years ago?
  Is theirs a well-run company? Are they proactive in improving?
- What are you most proud of in the area of benefits you provide to your employees? Why?
  What is their attitude about employees? Are they building loyalty and trust? Does their notion of what motivates people align with yours?
- Give us an example of a recommendation that a carrier made that had a positive impact.
  Do they partner with an agent? Are they open to suggestions and to change? Do they monitor their decisions?
- What changes in your industry would have the most marked effect on your profit margin?

Are they up to date? Are they market leaders? Do they analyze their finances effectively?

- If there were something to change to allow you to grow 15 percent, what would it be?
  Are they in a growth mode? Do the company's representatives share the corporate goals? How well can they articulate their opportunities?
- How has change in technology affected your business?
  Do they understand the impact of various technologies? How amenable might they be to new technologies that you could introduce? Are they market leaders or followers?
- Have you determined the difference between price and cost?
  Do they buy only commodities? Are they analytical about a value proposition?

Good Questions/Great Questions

There is a big difference between good questions and great questions. The foregoing are great questions because the answers help give you insight into what it would be like to do business with this whale.

Characteristics of Great Questions

- *Behavioral: What do you do when a project gets off track?*
- *Historical: How did this process work the last time?*
- *Specific: Who are the people that need to be involved?*
- *Narrative: Tell us about a great experience with a vendor?*
- *Comparative: How do you want your next experience to be different?*
- *Vulnerable: Give us an example of a project that you did not manage well.*
- *Predictive: What happens when we meet the first three benchmarks?*

Here are some specific examples of how to define a great question. Suppose you want to determine whether this prospect is a "price" buyer or a "value" buyer by asking, "Are you a price buyer or a value buyer?" Asking that question directly may not yield an answer. Instead, you could ask, "Tell me about one or two of the times in the last year that you made a buying decision for a product/service/contract as large as the one we are discussing where the final provider was not the lowest priced?" If they can't answer that question, or refuse to answer that question, you are learning a lot about them.

Another example is the issue of knowing whether the company is serious about changing suppliers. Ask them, "What was the process you used to bring on a significant new provider like us in the last two or three years, and how did it work out?" If they don't have an example or a process, you are learning a lot about your likelihood of success.

Early in the sales process, the harpooner should be all about asking great questions.

Avoid the Earn-It Trap

Often, we see companies get caught in what we call the *earn-it trap* when they are hunting whales. The earn-it trap is selling a small piece of work to a whale in the belief that it will lead to much bigger things. In our experience, this is a very low-yield strategy. Most of the time, if you go in through the small door, you get stuck in the little room. Why?

Let's look at this from a different angle. Suppose you were a qualified applicant for a senior position at a large company. Your resume, background, and education clearly put you in a position for a VP job. You go to the front door of the company, knock on it, and the person who answers the door has no idea which job might fit you and so sends you to human resources. At HR, you can interview for an open job in the mailroom because that is the problem HR has to solve today.

You don't want to be a mailroom clerk! Sigh. However, you do want to work at the big company. So you take the job. Time passes. Big jobs open, and other people are hired or promoted. Often, the person hired is both less qualified than you and from the outside.

You go to your boss and complain: "Hey, I am more qualified, I am a current employee, and I should be getting a shot at that job." Your boss tells you: (a) "You're doing a great job and we really need you where you are." (b) "I didn't know you had experience that qualified you for that job." (c) "Company policy is that you will have to submit an application like any other candidate from the outside and go through the same process." (d) All of the above.

How different is this approach faced by individuals from the earn-it approach faced by companies? Not very, but companies fall into the earn-it trap all the time. They take a little deal with a lot of hope and then they watch the big deals go to competitors. How can you avoid getting locked into the little room?

- *Knock on the right door.* Anyone who has landed a top job with a large company will tell you that the last door you knock on is human resources. Likewise, if you are at the procurement, diversity, or purchasing doors, you are starting at the wrong place. Deals end up here (after they are committed) to get the paperwork done, but they don't start here. You have to focus on the end-user door to get to the right person. Regardless of the whale's stated policy, if you start out in these areas, you have low potential for getting a whale-sized deal.

- *Leave the wrong room fast.* Sometimes, through good intentions from a friendly referral source, you end up at the wrong place. You know you are in the wrong place if you look around and there isn't an end user in the room. In our experience, trying to get directions from the wrong place to the right place rarely works. Better to stop, back up, and knock on a different door than to try to find the right door from the wrong room.
- *Beware of little nibbles with big promises.* If a whale-sized opportunity is real, there should be an adoption schedule with volume commitments based on performance standards for your firm to meet. If you hear, "We'll see how it goes," it is a sucker punch. If they have no plan, you have no path. No path means no commitment.

Here's an example. Our client, WorkPlace Media, is in the direct marketing business. Their unique capability is to place a retailer's discount coupon or special offer into an employee's paycheck, totally permission-based, and courtesy of the employer. Many national restaurant, retail, and consumer packaged goods companies engage the services of WorkPlace to drive traffic to their locations from at-work consumers on their way to work, at lunch, or on the drive home.

Typically, the whale (restaurant chain, for example) buys what is called a *test*. They authorize WorkPlace to distribute an offer within a specific geographic area, and if the test is successful, that should open the doors to more business, bigger business, and more extensive business. WorkPlace has performed exceptionally well on these tests. Yet often, when they returned to discuss more business and bigger business, they heard excuses from the whale. The metrics of success were under dispute. Or, yes, the test was successful, but, "We need to test again with a different offer." Or, most damaging of all, "Corporate sees this as a local strategy." It seemed as if the more successful they were, the more they were relegated to the small door, little room.

In the past, when the WorkPlace harpooners secured a meeting with a corporate representative, their history of success undermined them rather than positioning them for more and better business. The corporate buyers simply did not view the local or regional marketing buyers as dealing in the same universe. The corporate buying strategy did not have a budget for the services that WorkPlace provided, because they offer an innovative, entrepreneurial marketing model that blurs the lines between traditional media buys.

For these reasons, WorkPlace decided to markedly refocus their strategy, reposition their unique value proposition, and determine the criteria upon which they will say no thank you to the next offer of a local test unless all elements work in their favor. They have positioned themselves as "the expert in the behavior of the workplace consumer." They are taking this message to the corporate level, not only the local and regional levels, with increasing success. It takes guts and perseverance to make this kind of strategy change. But that's what whale hunting is all about.

To be fair, we have heard other owners of small to midsize businesses say that they have built their reputations and grown their businesses incrementally by selling a small deal to a whale, delivering excellent quality, and being invited to bid on larger jobs. In our experience, only manufacturing companies have made this tactic work. There's something about the delivery of a tangible product that meets or exceeds specs that induces the whale to buy more of the same. If it works, we are all for it. Still, we wonder if they have really positioned themselves as whale hunters, or are satisfied with a deal for 5 to 10 percent of the whale's product buy in a given year.

Back to Baja

One important lesson for your fast-growth company to learn is when to allow your whale-sized prospect to go "back to Baja" to be hunted another day. "Back to Baja" is a reference to the whales' migration patterns. Whales often live to be sixty years old. All of the whales that the Inuit did not capture in a single season would most likely return in subsequent years. The same principle holds true for whale-sized companies. They don't go out of business very often or very soon. They will still be good prospects next year or in three years or even five years.

Giving up on a sales prospect is one of the most difficult things to do for any ambitious entrepreneur, business manager, or salesperson. No one wants to give up on the sales process. Motivated business-people see a major prospect getting away and they often panic, making foolish moves or money-losing promises in an effort to resurrect the deal.

In most cases, these last-minute moves make no impact, often making your company look desperate. And even when these last gasps work to keep the deal alive, they can leave you with an unprofitable deal that can cost you more than profits. Losses often force you to cut back on services, leaving a bad relationship between you and the whale-sized client and assuring that you won't be doing future business with this important industry player.

How long do you pursue a deal before you move on to better immediate prospects? Take a lesson from the Inuit whale hunters. Early each spring they wait for the whales migrating up from Baja to their summer home in the far north. Early spring is the ideal time to hunt, as the whales pass close to the shore and the breaking ice floes help the hunters to confine their target.

The Inuit village does not expect to land all of the whales each year. They focus their energies on landing and harvesting one whale or a few whales, and they make a conscious decision not to be greedy. They study their prey. They know the natural seasons and cycles of the whale. They can afford to let a whale slip by on the journey north, because they know it will be on its way back soon. And they know that whales will be around for awhile.

Whale-sized customers have similar traits. They have cycles and seasons of buying. If they get "too far north," you will not capture them this year. It's imperative that you know when you've missed the whale in its current cycle, so that you don't waste time and resources on a lost cause.

Sending these whale prospects back to Baja is not just good sales practice; it is an essential business management practice for fast-growth firms. You can build your business exponentially by scouting, hunting, and harvesting a steady diet of whales-sized customers, but to do this you must study, learn, and document the business cycles of these profitable prospects. You must learn:

- Your prospect's buying season and cycles
- The signs of your prospect's readiness for a change
- The advance signs that will help you launch your hunting boat, or sales process, well before the prospect makes its buying decision
- The signs that the prospect has moved beyond your reach

This last point is the hardest to implement. Once you have a whale on your horizon, your harpooners will want to continue the hunt.

But the hunt is costly and dangerous, so smart villagers focus on the whale's long lifespan, protecting future selling opportunities.

Whale-sized companies might move away from you in their buying cycle, but they seldom disappear completely. While there are examples of huge companies going bankrupt or disappearing, this is rare. Whales are slow-moving but stable customers that provide multiple opportunities for patient hunters.

Place Your Bets

What if you think of each step in your whale hunting process as a $5,000 bet? It will change your perception of the cost of the sales process. Most companies account for their sales expense as overhead or G&A expense. This method can hide the true expense of your organization's technical, operational, and other departmental resources because it does not vary based on the likelihood of closing.

And if you add in the opportunity cost and direct sales expense, $5,000 per step is probably a low number. Just look at these typical steps in a simple sales process: qualify, first meeting, presentation/demo, proof of concept/prototype, and proposal. In a whale-sized deal, if each step is a $5,000 bet, you would have $25,000 on the table at the point of a proposal. Plenty of whales will let you get all the way to proposal with little possibility of your getting the business. Why shouldn't they? It's not their money. But if you had to write a $5,000 check every time you took a step, you would be much more deliberate in deciding whether the next step was worth the bet.

If the buying process is being dictated by procurement or purchasing, and you do not have access to the end buyers in the process, play *only* if you know you are the lowest-cost provider. You will spend a lot of expensive time in the RFQ/RFP process. Coming in through the door marked "Procurement" and hoping to be the "value provider," is naïve, wasteful, and against all odds of your success.

Use your target filter to remain focused on the characteristics of your ideal whales. If too many characteristics are outside of your filter, you will spend big money to lose the deal. Practice saying no.

Exercise your choice. In the sales process, too often we get committed to taking the next step just because we have taken the previous step. A first appointment leads us to the expectation of a second appointment, which leads to a presentation or demo, which leads to a quote. Isn't that the sales process? Not if you think of every step as a $5,000 bet.

Don't be the pigeon. Lots of whales will include multiple companies in a sales process even when they have no interest in moving the business from their current provider. Often, they just want to educate themselves on the market and to beat up their current vendor on price. If you can't figure out early in the process why the whale is really going to move the business to you, chances are it won't.

Whale hunting is gutsy, calculated, and expensive. You have to pay to play, so you ought to play only to win.

Fish along the Way

If your target filter is constructed correctly, it might pass through 99 percent of the whale-sized companies. Seeing these valuable whales swimming into the sunset usually concerns companies that are whale hunting for the first time. They worry that their sales pipelines will empty out and that no money will come in while they hunt for the right whale.

But just as the crew of an Inuit boat will fish for food as they pursue their whale, you will undoubtedly continue some of your usual sales procedures while you perfect new whale hunting process. We do, however, recommend a strategy whereby you will deliberately cease to do business with the lowest 10 percent of your business every year.

How do we define the lowest 10 percent? It may represent the lowest margin. Perhaps it is the top 10 most difficult customers to satisfy. Maybe it's the hardest from whom to collect. Chances are, everyone in your village knows the customers they would love to dump. They drain energy. They don't value who you are or the products or services you supply. They don't challenge you to grow with them. Perhaps they demand repeated cost cuts and service increases. They refuse to understand how your business model and product offerings are advancing and growing more sophisticated. Despite perhaps a long relationship, they see you only the "way you were" in relationship to them.

You have to feed your village. Catch fish and small game as you need to keep the village fed. But begin the process of freeing resources for a whale hunt by making more deliberate and strategic decisions about the fishing.

The question is when and how are you going expend the time, talent, and cost of hunting a whale-sized prospect. Save those expenditures for whales. Fish for your present needs, but hunt whales for your future.

As the harpooner, when you have gained the attention of a whale that seems well suited to your village, it becomes your responsibility to populate your boat with oarsmen—subject matter experts—who will support your leadership in completing a sale to the whale. In the next chapter, we describe the process of that hunt.

Set the Harpoon Action Items

- *Plan the harpooning process with a focus on your initial contacts with the whale.*
- *Control the aperture of perception to manage the whale's confidence about your company.*
- *Go in the right door where you can discuss a whale-sized deal.*
- *Ask great questions of the buyers' table.*
- *Send a whale "back to Baja" when your timing is not right.*
- *Fish along the way so as to feed your village.*

Please visit www.thewhalehunters.com to download the sales process tools introduced in this chapter.

6

Ride the Whale

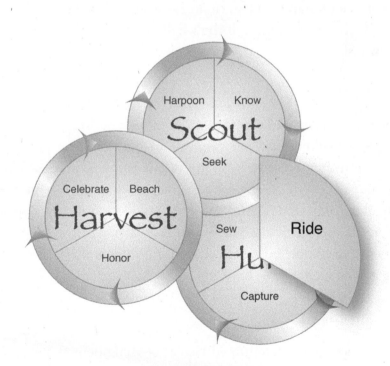

ONCE THE HARPOON HAD BEEN SET, the whale took off—it dived, it swam, it contorted. It certainly didn't give up. The Inuit hunters hung on tight to the rope and worked to tire the whale. They used tools to slow it down—bladders filled with water, for example—yet because of the whale's size, speed, and intelligence, it was extremely difficult to land.

The ride could be dangerously long. The whale could pull the tiny boat and crew into unfamiliar waters, far from shore and far from the resources of the village. Hunters could become entangled in the rope or jettisoned onto floating ice. The worst outcome would be to endure the pain and fear of the ride, to lose tools and equipment or, more significantly, hunters—and still fail to land the whale. We can be certain that the whale hunters were very focused on their task.

The Hunt

Riding the whale marks a transition from scouting (the phases of knowing, seeking and harpooning) to hunting (the phases of riding, capturing, and sewing) in the Whale Hunters' Process. Until now, you've been learning, about your capabilities, about your ocean, about the whales. And you've sent a harpooner out to learn more about a particular whale and to get that whale's attention. When you've completed all of the scouting work and you've set the harpoon, you are ready to hunt in earnest.

Launch a Boat

Your harpooner has determined that the whale demonstrates the characteristics of a good prospect. One or more people on the buyers' side have demonstrated interest, continued communication, and some degree of readiness. When all the initial signals look positive, it is time for the shaman or company leadership team to launch a boat to pursue a deal with this whale.

We use the analogy of "the boat" to define the team of subject matter experts (SMEs) from your company who will participate in the hunt for a particular whale. Throughout this chapter, we will offer examples and illustrations about how you will select subject matter experts, how you will train and prepare them, and what value you will gain by launching a boat rather than sending out a lone hunter.

By "launching a boat," we mean committing the attention and resources to pursue this whale actively and with single-minded intention to land the deal. Not only are you committing sales force resources to this deal, but the shaman and harpooner will borrow personnel from other areas of the company—engineering, IT, human resources, customer service, manufacturing, warehousing, installation—depending on the nature of your business and the complexity of your sale. So before you launch, you need to be able to answer three questions affirmatively:

- Are the odds of landing this deal in our favor? Based upon your scouting knowledge and the harpooner's initial contacts, the prospect is probably going to buy something, has a budget to buy, and is willing to consider buying from you.
- Can we commit adequate resources to ensure a successful hunt? The harpooner and shaman will devote full attention to the hunt. Several subject matter experts will help to plan, prepare, and take part in meetings or other events. You may decide to host an event at your location to demonstrate your capabilities to this prospect. It can be expensive to do that well.

- Can we harvest this whale if we land it? By definition, whale-sized deals transform your company. With careful planning and preparation, and as you transition from an occasional whale to a steady diet of whales, the exceptional big deal becomes routine. But early in the whale hunting process, be certain that you are willing to invest in the operations, equipment, delivery, and ancillary services that the whale might require.

Once you decide to launch a boat, you have a series of processes to invent and process decisions to formulate:

- Your whale hunting process steps
- Your understanding of the whale
- Your training of your team

In actual practice, these are parallel needs and activities. We will develop these practices in this and successive chapters. In this chapter, we will focus on how your team learns to understand the buyer, and prepare to engage with the buyer in substantive, pertinent, and well-orchestrated encounters.

The Buyers' Table

Big companies don't buy one to one on a big-deal purchase. They have a team of buyers. They want to spread out the risk and responsibility of buying and be certain that all areas that might be affected by a change in vendor or the purchase of a new product or service have been consulted. *Misunderstanding this process is a key mistake that small companies make in trying to sell to big companies.* Your company's executive team, the shaman, and the harpooner are all responsible for understanding how this works and learning specifically who all the buyers will be. The better you become at understanding the buyers, the more successfully you will hunt.

We visualize the team of buyers as the "buyers' table." At times during the sales process, you are literally "at the table" with the buyers. At other times, people from your team and their team are meeting separately, talking by phone, exchanging emails, or introducing additional buyers and sellers into the process.

At every point of contact, you need to ensure that all members of your team are engaging appropriately, professionally, and knowledgeably with their counterparts. Managing the sales process at this level of specificity offers you big advantages in closing big accounts. You are not hunting just to hunt; you are hunting to land this whale.

We identify two types of buyers who will show up at the buyers' table on a big deal. They are:

- *Financial buyer:* The person who has the ultimate authority to commit the whale's money to doing business with you; the one who can say yes.
- *Specialized buyers:* People from a variety of departments that may be affected by a decision to purchase from you. None of these buyers can say yes to a deal but any one of them can say no.

We say that the specialized buyers can say no because the financial buyer does not want to make a decision that will not be embraced by other members of the team. Here's an example. Our client, Six Disciplines Leadership Center of Central Indiana, offers professional business improvement services. At the beginning of the sales process, they talk to CEOs, founders, owners, partners—each of whom is a financial buyer. But none of these buyers will buy

Six Discipline's services unless other members of the management team are in accord, including, in particular, the CFO, the COO, and the CIO.

Post a chart of the buyers' table in your offices. Circulate it among the members of your boat. Continue to populate it with names and titles. Determine who in your boat can best relate to each buyer, adding new subject matter experts if need be.

Here's an example of a buyers' table form. Those seated on the whale's side of the table fulfill a variety of roles. Someone at the table has the ultimate power to say yes to you. You may not meet that person until later in the process. More important, many people have the power to say no. The ultimate buyer is unlikely to buy from you unless the entire buyers' table is satisfied with you, your product, your service, your price, your promises.

The Buyers' Table

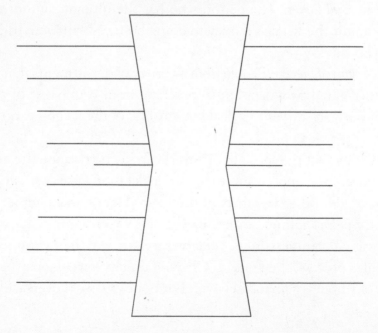

Small companies often think that the purpose of all these buyers is to ensure that the whale chooses the best possible supplier. Actually, the purpose is to avoid making a bad decision. That's the most important point for you to understand, because it is what makes you—a smaller company—vulnerable in doing a deal with a big company.

Here's an example. Our client, Crew Technical Services, was an outsourced provider of engineering validation services, doing about 80 percent of its business with a single whale and desirous of diversifying both its services and its clientele. Crew had developed a notable capacity for technical writing, and through its chart the waters activity determined that state government would make an excellent whale, with many upcoming needs for big technical writing contracts, such as revising all of the state's motor vehicle handbooks.

As Crew studied the buyers' table, they realized that they did not know any specialized buyers in state government. Their two harpooners had done a good job of getting to know agency heads and members of state government who might be influential in vendor selection. Crew's chief was actively engaged in those meetings with key counterparts. But what were the specialized buyers thinking? Who would be advising the agency head on a final selection? Which preferred vendors did they already have in mind? What were their fears about a new vendor with which they would have to work on a daily basis?

Crew embarked on a systematic effort to get to know all the buyers in the key state agencies where they wanted to bid. They introduced members of their management team. For example:

"This is the person who manages our technical writing services; she will manage all of the employees who will work on your project."

"Please meet the person who is responsible for the final accuracy of our products; she can tell you how we control documents and manage proofreading."

"I'd like you to meet the person who manages our information technology; he can talk to your IT team about the security of your data and our transfer of completed documents to your system."

In this way, Crew became a trusted provider of technical writing services to a new whale, achieving their objectives of growing their business, building a new service line, and reducing their reliance on one customer.

Big Companies/Small Companies

Why do big companies like to do business with other big companies? Our clients identify a number of factors, including these:

- Reputation
- Stability
- Prestige
- Speak the same language
- Similar systems and processes
- No one gets blamed for the decision

Why do big companies like to do business with small companies? See if these reasons are on your list:

- Control
- Agility and flexibility

- Possibly price
- Attention from the top
- Innovation
- Concessions

The items on the first list are all about the whale's fear. But the items on the second list are all about advantage. If you can overcome the whale's fear, you can win the deal with your advantages. But all the advantages on earth will not help if you do not have a system for overcoming whales' fear.

It is hard to believe you could scare a whale. Whales are huge, strong, and much more powerful than you are, right? But when you look into the culture of a whale-sized organization, you may find a fearful place harboring fearful people. They scare easily, so your job is to alleviate their fear.

Whale cultures can be maddening to smaller, more entrepreneurial companies, How many times have you been selling into a whale-sized company and left meetings or phone calls shaking your head because the buyers could not or would not make a decision that was so clearly in their company's best interests? How can you explain their reluctance? How can you bring them to a decision?

The nature of whales is to seek safety over benefit. For that reason, fear trumps all other emotions in their process of making a decision. Smaller companies that sell to whales usually tout the benefits that they will provide, with little attention to the whale's fears. Therefore, they often make mistakes during their sales process that create more fear in the whale and lead to unsuccessful hunts. To hunt more successfully, you must learn how to stop scaring whales.

What Whales Fear

- Change: *Any variation from what they are doing now*
- Conflict: *Any disruption of the relationships, inter- or intradepartmental, between the whale and customers or current suppliers*
- Work: *Any additional expenditure of effort or activity in the current workload of the people with whom you are meeting*
- Failure: *Mistakes, shortcomings, problems, or any other public signs of a bad decision*

Do you feel stuck here? If you are selling anything significant (typical of a whale-sized deal), you inevitably create at least one of these circumstances, and usually more than one. From a whale hunting perspective, you need specific tactics to reduce the whale's fears so that the whale can be ready to hear your benefits. Here are our recommendations to counter fear and move toward advantage:

1. *Get everyone to the buyers' table*. Everyone who will be impacted by the whale's buying decision must be at the table, since you cannot educate or calm people with whom you are not connected. If any department or group may be impacted negatively by working with your company, it is better to hear them out and work through the issues than to avoid their concerns.

2. *Devote 90:10 effort to a 50:50 commitment*. Declare early and often that if the whale will make its portion of the commitment, you will take more than your share of the implementation responsibility. You might offer to provide extra training resources from your company, backup tooling and engineering, or delivery schedules that are outside of your normal way of doing business. Regardless of what it is, you have to be able to

show the buyers that the effort on your side will be enough to take a lot of the transition burden off of them.

3. *Reinforce the status quo.* Make certain that the whale clearly understands which of its many systems will *not* change as a consequence of doing a deal with you. All complex systems, such as accounting, procurement, supply chain management, training, manufacturing, and so on, require a great deal of effort to modify, as well as great risk of interruption if something does not work. Highlight regularly how your solution will *not* change these systems, and you will make the whale feel more at ease with you.

4. *Propose specific steps in the comprehensive plan.* Build a plan with incremental ramp-in and clearly defined performance thresholds for continuing and growing the relationship.

5. *Spread it out.* Demonstrate that you can dedicate more people, more resources, and more time than your competitors. In considering a purchase from a smaller company, the whale likes the idea that it will have leverage in the relationship, as well as access to your company's best and brightest. However, it also fears that your company might be too small to deliver. Showing the strength of your people, your resources, and your time commitments during the sales process will help the whale to feel comfortable in choosing to do business with you.

Finally, try asking these questions to get the whale's fears out on the table early.

- If we were signing the contract to do work together today, who from your company would have to be in the room?
- Who in your company might be negatively impacted if you changed what you are doing now and started using us?

- Tell me about the on-boarding of the last provider/partner/vendor/supplier to your company from the outside, and what were the major issues?
- When you have worked with firms like ours in the past, what snafus have you had to deal with? How can you guide us to avoid those mistakes?

Their answers should guide your sales plan. You will know who needs to be at the buyers' table, which departments have the most to lose, how to calm their fears about problems in the past, and what their biggest fears are about buying from a small company. You are smaller than a whale, and that size differential is what most scares the whale in a business dealing with you.

Fear Busters

Now that you know the whale is afraid of you, it's time to marshal your "fear-busting" tactics. Always calm the whale's fears with one or more of the following:

- Your people: knowledgeable, capable, competent, accessible
- Your technology: up to date, reliable, easy to integrate and to use
- Your processes: manageable, measurable, replicable
- Your experience: references, examples, and case studies

First, identify the tools that you have currently that could help in relieving the prospect's fears. We use a chart such as the one shown in Table 6.1.

Table 6.1 Fear-Buster Tools			
Generic Whale Fears	**Specific Whale Fear about You**	**Current Tools Used to Alleviate Whale Fear**	**Current Tool Rating Weak/ Neutral/Positive**
Change			
Conflict			
Mistakes			
Work			

As you fill out the chart, identify first the ways in which you might provoke fear in the whale, for example:

- Fear of change, perhaps caused by:
  - Paperwork
  - Systems
  - Training
  - Personnel
- Fear of conflict, perhaps with the:
  - End user
  - Customer
  - Subcontractors
- Fear of mistakes, such as:
  - Ours
  - Theirs—Will we cover for them?
  - Price—Will they pay too much?

- Fear of work, including:
  - How we will work with them
  - How much new work will our contract entail?

Table 6.2 shows a specific client example, modified to protect proprietary information.

When you have analyzed the specific ways in which you might scare this whale, you can begin to identify your fear-buster tools. What are you doing today to alleviate those fears?

Finally, rate your current fear busters—are they okay, are they weak, are they great? This exercise will identify gaps in your presentation and prompt you to know the people who should populate your boat, and the processes, experience, and technologies they should present.

Power Your Boat

Before you set out on the ocean, riding your whale, it is time to make sure you are working with the most powerful boat possible. What kind of boat are you working with? A Windsurfer? A dinghy? A Sunfish sailboat?

You could ride a whale with any of these types of boats, but do you want to? Wouldn't you rather hunt from a power boat? This conjures up pictures of strength, control, and ultimately victory.

The Inuit umiak was not a motorized boat, but it was nevertheless powerful. It relied on the concerted, orchestrated efforts of a select team whose members had been provided with the village's best wisdom, tools, supplies, and support. Likewise, you can choose a fine team for your hunt, but selecting the team members is not enough; you need to equip them to fulfill their roles and work together.

Table 6.2 Whale Fear Example

Fear	Specific Whale Fear	Tool Used to Address	Rating
Safety	Lack of experience Auditing	Web site sample, client list, 12 case studies, 4 pages of testimonials	+
		Gaps in info for new markets	− (for new markets)
		Coverage map— actually hit business	+
Resources	Doubt our capabilities: people, facility, industry knowledge, money to offset mistakes	Client list—samples	0
		"Breadth of what we do" chart	−
		Leverage the 19 years	+
		Insurance certificate	+
		Run a D&B	+
Brand/Message	Never heard of us; lack of competition; no benchmarks; don't want to be first	Testimonials Press releases Ads Case studies Survey results Radio interviews on Web site	− to 0
Always done it this way	Resistance to change; decision-maker's personal risk	Testimonials Case studies Selling the value of the audience Selling the channel Decision-maker success	− to 0
Scalable	Too small to handle business	Predictive modeling Agency testimonials, list of agencies	−
Longevity	Perception of no "real" experience		

Power your boat by equipping everyone to perform at his or her optimum level. We have identified five power principles for a victorious whale-hunting boat.

- *Understand power positions within the whale.* The power position in the whale is usually not the person who can say yes but rather the people who can say no (the specialists: operational, technical, and financial people). If you have launched a boat, you know that your champion in the whale is already excited by the "why you" answers you have given. Now, using the boat, you have to prove that working with your company will be safe at the day-to-day, operational level. In other words, you need to make certain that your people are capable of demonstrating the what and the how of your solution.
- *Use power tools during your ride.* Make the whale comfortable working with your company. The whale wants control and needs a sense of safety. Savvy buyers know that there will be occasional undertows and squalls. Don't pretend that there will not be problems. Demonstrate how your company will work through problems and resolve issues. Visual and physical examples are powerful tools. Use reports. Show the regular reporting information and ongoing performance monitoring that you will provide. Be certain that the customer will always know how things are going and how you will manage exceptions. Use samples and demonstrations. If you use software to track activity and progress, show it. If you use special quality measurement equipment, demonstrate it. If a process you use reduces any form of risk, walk through it with whale representatives, and illustrate every step.

- *Make and show a "you are here" map.* Think of the "you are here" map at any shopping mall or airport kiosk. Every member of the buyers' table prefers a *personal* map that walks him or her through every step of how you will work together. It is not enough to tell. You must show. People need a very clear illustration— focused on their personal experience—of how they will work with you. Be prepared to demonstrate your tools regularly and repetitively throughout the process to increase the whale's sense of confidence. You are trying to convey a sense of safety to every member of the buyers' table.

- *Make power statements.* There are hundreds of good things about your company, your service or product, and your solution. But if you try to tell all of them, you will lose the buyers' attention and dilute the high-leverage advantages that matter most. Select no more than three appropriate and significant points for each member of your boat to present. Work through the language with each member so that everyone is comfortable making the power statements and confident about how these key benefits contribute value to the whale. Clarify that each member of your boat understands who at the buyers' table will be most interested in and influenced by their presentation.

- *Ask power questions.* Probing, pertinent questions are powerful. The buyers respond, your team gains knowledge, and you learn how best to tailor your discussion to the whale's specific issues. However, questions can hurt you if they reveal that a member of your boat is not knowledgeable about the prospective customer. Inappropriate questions bring the discussion to a grinding halt and frustrate everyone on the whale's team.

Be certain that everyone on your team is prepared with the right kinds of questions and has been instructed to avoid the wrong ones.

Inappropriate Questions

- Lack of coordination questions. *Questions that have already been answered for some members of your team but not shared with others demonstrate a lack of process and knowledge sharing.*
- Lack of preparation questions. *Questions about the whale that your team should have learned through advance research indicate laziness and shallowness on your part.*
- Lack of knowledge questions. *Questions about the whale's industry and competitive environment, which your company is required to understand, leave the whale questioning your suitability as a partner.*

Whale hunting demands power. You can power your boat by equipping all members of the team with an understanding of the sales context, with specific tools by which they can demonstrate your company's value, with key points of differentiation between you and your competitors, and with meaningful questions to engage your prospect in joint decision making with you.

Rules of the Boat

If you've spent any time on a boat, you know there are rules. On a sailboat, duck when the boom comes across. On a power boat, stay in your seat. On a pontoon, don't all move to the port side at once. On a canoe, keep your balance. If you violate the rules, you can get hurt and put others in jeopardy. We need rules to keep the boat functioning. And we need rules because boats are subject to forces beyond the crew's control—wind, tides, storms, traffic—even pirates and hijackers. A successful crew knows the rules, rehearses its roles, and prepares for the unknown.

The Inuit whale hunters launched a boat—an umiak with an eight-man crew—to hunt a whale. Likewise, we use the analogy of launching a boat to express a modern company's decision to pursue a whale-sized deal. A whale hunt is expensive and dangerous, so you need to consider carefully all of the steps in your process.

We offer eight rules for a contemporary whale-hunt launch.

1. *Prepare your boat.* Launching the boat means that your team and the whale's team will meet face to face for a presentation, whether at your place or theirs. Your team needs to match up appropriately with members of the buyers' group. Decide each boat member's role, determine his or her match-up in the whale, define the meeting plan, and rehearse who will say what and when. Consider also with your crew what you will do if the whale violently bolts from the agenda and takes you out into different waters.
2. *Control the agenda.* Just as the wise captain reads the charts, you should chart your meeting. Take the responsibility to create and send an agenda. List all participants, with titles, from your company and the whale's company. Declare a purpose for the meeting. Identify up to five discussion topics. Define the desired outcomes. Provide all attendees with a list of and links to all relevant documentation. In other words, be in charge.
3. *Take enough oarsmen.* When smaller companies do business with whales, they are tempted to use the same sales process that has been successful in the past—that is, a key salesperson or two-person team. But if you cannot match up with the team

around the buyers' table, you will appear too small. Of course, if you take too many people, you look a little desperate. We recommend the ratio of two boat members for every three people you are meeting from the whale organization.

4. *Show up "warm."* Once you acquire the contact information for all of the attendees, find a reason to call a few days before the meeting. Ask a question, confirm a piece of information, suggest a data point that you think might be valuable, validate your understanding of an existing system or process that the whale is using—anything that makes sense. Make certain that someone from your company has made some contact with the meeting attendees in advance so that the meeting is warm at the start. You will gather important information and good impressions if you follow this rule.

5. *Set the table.* Emily Post, Dear Abby, and your mom have coached you on seating your guests. Allowing your team to sit on one side of the table, across from "them," is not an arrange-ment for building trust and interaction. Determine who you want sitting next to whom, and then make certain to get the meeting table set that way. If you are hosting the meeting, use place cards, or seat your guests deliberately. If the meeting is in the whale's office, as the meeting is opening and everyone is shaking hands, have your match-ups take their counterparts and sit next to them. It really is that simple, if you are deter-mined in advance. Now you have proximity and the opportu-nity for peer-to-peer conversations throughout the meeting.

6. *Own the next steps.* Make it clear that someone on your team will take notes and circulate them to all of the attendees. This practice is courteous, ensures that you have documentation, and creates another reason to reconnect with the whale

attendees after the meeting. This responsibility should include capturing both companies' assignments and scheduling the follow-up meeting.

7. *Open with expectations and close with summaries.* Every attendee from the whale comes to each meeting with a key agenda item. Why guess what the issues are? Instead, open each meeting with a simple question to the group—for example, "What is the most important issue that each of you would like addressed in today's discussion?" Capture each item on paper, and at the end of the meeting, review the items out loud one by one to make certain that the author of the item has been satisfied. Include these points in your documentation.

8. *Debrief and learn.* After every meeting, every conference call, every trade show—every, every, every time—get your boat together and ask the simple questions. What worked well that we can leverage next time? What can we do better next time? Write these answers down and share them with all of your boats. If you want to become overwhelmingly effective in hunting whales, these two questions are your guides.

Your company can become expert in launching and sailing your boat. You can learn more about your whales, better prepare to serve their needs, and grow your revenues.

While the riding phase of whale hunting takes patience, it can be a rewarding time. One positive aspect of riding is that it is a time when real transformation can occur. The teamwork and quick decision making that is required to stay with the whale can change a company that has fallen into bad habits into a hungry, tightly run firm constantly on the lookout for new whales. Whale hunting leads to a new level of accountability and contribution as employees never before involved in the sales process find themselves an integral part of future growth.

First, you located your whale. Then you harpooned it by convincing primary decision makers within the whale-sized prospect of your capability to supply their needs in a unique fashion. Then you began riding it, making sure that the entire chain of buyers within the whale understood your message and bought in to your unique abilities. Now the whale is showing signs of giving up its fight. You must be preparing for the next phase. It is time to complete the *capture*.

Ride the Whale Action Items

- *Launch a boat with adequate resources to land the whale.*
- *Analyze the buyers' table to understand the whale's fears and define your fear busters.*
- *Power your boat by equipping subject matter experts with great questions, training them to perform, and rehearsing their performance.*
- *Create metrics for the boat's performance.*

Please visit www.thewhalehunters.com to download the sales process tools introduced in this chapter.

7

Capture the Whale

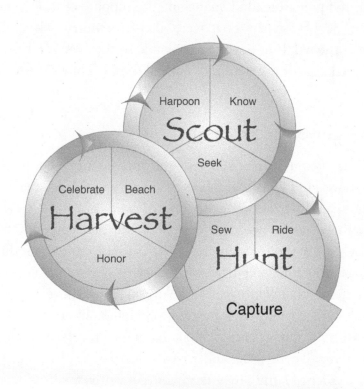

SUDDENLY THE WHALE BEGAN to relinquish. After a wild and tortuous ride, with the umiak seemingly at the mercy of the whale, all at once the boat began to gain the upper hand. By means of a reliable process, excellent tools, superior knowledge, and demonstrable courage, the umiak started to direct its own course. The whale ceased to fight, and the boat was able to tow the whale rather than to follow the whale's lead.

Of course, with a whale in tow, the boat had to constantly calibrate its progress. It had to use the winds and the tides, as well as oars, to steer in what the team believed to be the right direction. All of the oarsmen were busy with their usual tasks—minding the line, fishing and preparing food, managing the supplies of fresh water.

The people on the boat were also in a hurry. They wanted to beach the whale as quickly as possible so they wouldn't lose it to other predators or the whims of natural forces. They were focused.

Map Your Sales Process

In the last chapter, we talked about how to organize your team for a whale hunt, and specifically how to prepare each member to contribute in a significant and appropriate way.

In this chapter, we cover some of the same ground, but we approach it from the standpoint of the chronology of the individual steps and the time frame within which you want to accomplish each step. In other words, we are looking at how to develop your specific sales process map for hunting your whales. To create your map, begin with the phases of the Whale Hunters' Process. These remain constant for all companies and across industries. Within each phase, begin to identify the steps that you currently take, or that you will begin taking as you implement whale hunting.

We will present three examples from our clients who have developed very successful whale-hunting maps. We will discuss the qualities of those maps and how they work to make the hunt more successful.

The change from riding to capturing your whale might begin so gradually that it is almost imperceptible. Or it might start with a bang of cooperation and coordination. Whatever the impetus, capturing a whale-sized deal is not like signing one of your regular customers. It isn't a "transactional close" marked by signing on the dotted line to buy a car. You aren't looking for a simple yes, a handshake, and the signing of a contract. In fact, you must be leery if things begin moving too rapidly.

Progressive Discovery, Progressive Disclosure

In a traditional sales process, the salesperson overwhelms the prospect with all of the advantages his or her company can offer and all the benefits the buyer can receive. That kind of selling is *telling*—whoever you want us to be, that's who we are. We're big, or we're small. We're inexpensive, or we're more expensive but worth it. We provide an off-the-shelf turnkey solution, but we can customize if that's what you want. The selling company's fear is that it will miss an opportunity for which it could have provided a product or service.

Whale hunting is completely different. It works from the premise that you have a carefully crafted, limited, powerful message that is not for every buyer but is designed to be perfect for some key big-account buyers. The role of *listening* becomes paramount. The ability to ask powerful questions, to listen carefully to the answers, and to craft that information into a winning proposal are core attributes of a company that successfully hunts whales.

We think of the sales process for a complex sale as a series of *discoveries* and *disclosures*. That is, you determine a plan for what you want to discover from your prospect at every step of the process. Likewise, you determine a plan for what you will disclose at each step. Contrary to the traditional model, we advocate that you encourage the whale to share more information earlier in the sales process, while you share more information later in the process.

The sales process that we recommend, then, develops the twin concepts of *discover* and *disclose*. Two sets of knowledge and competency drive that process:

1. You learn how to understand and to map the buyers' table. You developed that understanding in the previous chapter, and now you know those who are at the buyers' table and how each member of your boat will interact with them. Each whale presents a different buyers' table, but the process by which you learn about it will become standard and repeatable in your organization.
2. You define your steps in terms of what you want to learn, what you want to teach, and who needs to be involved in your process along the way.

Throughout the hunt, the harpooner now becomes the choreographer of a cross-functional team, managing the flow of information, directing the interaction between your company and the whale, and monitoring progress—in general, steering "the boat."

Identifying the steps of your *progressive discovery* and *progressive disclosure* marks a good place to start developing a sales process map. The sample chart shown here offers a place to record: (1) the questions that you will ask at each stage of the process; (2) the information that you will reveal at each stage of the process; and (3) the forms, templates, and tools that you characteristically use in your whale-hunting process.

Progressive Discovery/Disclosure

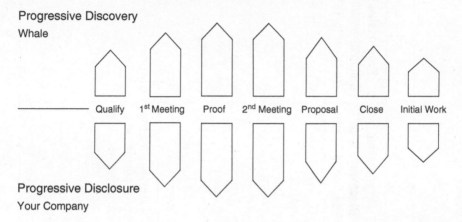

As we work with our clients, we post a big diagram of this process on a wall. The cross-functional team—what we call the "boat"—identifies the questions that they want to ask and the answers that they have to have at every step of the process. In the first iteration of building this map, everyone posts sticky notes about questions, answers, challenges, and concerns. After the first collaborative process event, team leadership organizes the ideas and information into the first-draft sales process map. As teams begin to use the map, more opportunities are presented to learn and revise. The sales process map becomes a work in progress, subject to continual revision and improvement as your organization learns.

Our client, Power Direct, is adept at the sales process mapping. Table 7.1 is an excerpt from a draft document they developed to map their steps in progressive discovery and progressive disclosure. This chart began as a big wall document and was summarized into the draft sales process map. Your list should include the steps that have gone into successful sales of the past big deals, always subject

Table 7.1 Draft Sales Process Map

Step	Who from Power Direct	Who from the Whale	Progressive Discovery (What We Want to Learn)	Progressive Disclosure (What We Want to Tell)
First qualify	VP, business development (BD)	VP, marketing/sales/ vendor relations	Answer target filter questions. Look for whale signs. Find the right contacts.	We know your markets.
Interest	VP, BD	VP, marketing/sales/ vendor relations	What needs What markets Describe your past channel experiences/ failures.	Web site PowerPoint Case studies
Second qualify	VP, BD Two-plus senior management	VP, marketing/sales/ vendor relations	First follow-up meeting Specific program needs and requirements Potential size/growth potential Timing requirements/ capacity Budget specifics	References Capabilities

Launch the boat	CEO—Launch: yes or no? Identify our team	None		Launch: yes or no?
Visit them	COO CIO CEO VP, BD	CIO COO VP, sales/marketing Quality/reporting	Prequalify who's at the table Fact-finding mission Terms of engagement	Our SMEs—put a face to them Quality control and compliance—fear-driven questions Timing Capacity Ramp-up
Visit us	COO/Operations CIO CEO VP, BD Services Quality Training Supervisors Compliance HR	Same-level individuals	Previsit meeting (internally) Set agenda according to their needs Who are they bringing? Technical requirements	Right people with their buyers Speak to their needs Tour Counterparts introduced Setup meeting/checklist How we manage intake? How to work with us?

to revision. Depending on the nature of your business, steps might include such things as:

1. Qualify the prospect.
2. Develop a product prototype.
3. Get prospect approval of scope of the project.
4. Agree on a contract.
5. Arrange terms.

The initial value of the sales map is that you have the steps in writing where they can be easily communicated to each member of the crew. As you have future successes, the items on the map will change, but don't wait to draw a map until you feel your process is perfect. It is important to have something down on paper. Otherwise, you are rudderless in dangerous water.

Working from this draft map, the Power Direct team knows who needs to be engaged at each step of their sales process, what they want to learn, and what they want to present. They have a basis for preparing one another for face-to-face meetings with the buyers' table and for preparing and revising their key sales documents. The harpooner will have detailed information to present to the CEO in advance of the decision to launch a boat for any whale.

The sales process map varies widely depending on your industry or type of business. The Whale Hunters have worked with companies that have as few as 10 steps in their sales process to firms with as many as 39 steps. It's most important to capture the steps that will be significant to your company in selling a big deal to a big client. The illustration here is another method of representing the map, in this case a visual form created by our client, Ontario Systems. This is an excerpt from only one phase of the Whale Hunters' Process.

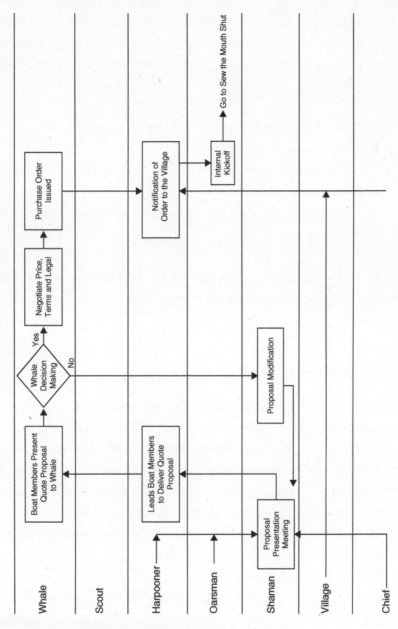

Capturing the Whale

This map indicates an owner or a specific person responsible for each step. It works well as a visual image posted prominently for members of the boat and the village to consult. Your map also needs a list of:

- Roles and responsibilities for every participant
- Resources needed for each step
- Subprocesses or discrete moves that need to be made to successfully complete steps like the contract
- Success criteria so that the organization knows when to move to the next step.

In addition, the map should contain a timeline with estimates of how long each step should require. We provide a more detailed map later.

Time Kills All Deals

The next most important task in your mapping process is to assign a recommended time frame to each step. How long should it take for you and the prospect to complete each step in your sales process?

One of our favorite clients coined the term "darn-near-done-deal" (DNDD). Yes, we can hear you laughing. Anyone who has ever sold anything understands that awful space between "darn near done" and "sold." And all the myriad ways we convince ourselves that a dead deal is an almost-done deal!

The salespeople/harpooners express eternal optimism about deals. They need a process to save them from their own enthusiasm. The entrepreneurial founder/chief frequently shares an unwarranted optimism with the harpooners. After all, they have a shared history of closing long-shot deals, extraordinary deals, wonderful and amazing deals. On the other hand, the CFO and the COO may take a jaundiced attitude toward the *deal flow,* believing that you close a far lower percentage of deals than your history would suggest. And if you are like many of our clients, you don't really know how long it takes, on average, to close a big deal—and you particularly don't know how long it takes from one step to the next. Anecdotes and rock-star stories will not substitute for data.

As you begin to define your whale hunting process steps, you need to assign a time frame to each one. If you have any historical data about the steps in your sales process, now is the time to use it as a starting point. But at first, these may be purely arbitrary time frames, based on some rule of thumb or even what you hope will be the case. Learning what the time frame should be represents a great advantage that accrues to those who implement a step-by-step process and attempt to assign time durations to each step.

Table 7.2 illustrates another way of representing the sales process map, from Ontario Systems. It indicates core criteria for the steps ride, capture, and sew in the Whale Hunters' Process, and represents in greater detail the process flowchart map shown earlier in this chapter.

This map provides a detailed management plan. Not only does it stipulate what needs to happen and who is responsible for making it happen, it also provides a reference for how much time is allotted for the completion of each step in the process. For example, look at steps 13 and 14. The shaman has allocated the harpooner 14 days to prepare and present the company's proposal. The whale is allowed 21 days to reach a decision about the proposal.

But suppose the whale doesn't respond in 21 days? After all, your harpooners can't control the whale's time frame, can they?

Table 7.2 Alternative Sales Process Map

Phase	Step	Description	Timeline	Owner	Roles	Resources	Metric
Ride	8	Discovery— send planning guide	1 day	Harpooner	Project manager	Standard planning guide	Customer verifies
	9	Web overview session	1 day	Harpooner	Training	WebEx presentation	Completion
	10	On-site requirements analysis	4 days	Harpooner	Project manager	Question- naires, interviews	Visit completed
	11	Request specification documents	21 days	Harpooner	Project manager	Reports from on-site visit	RSD report completed
	12	Develop the quotation	7 days	Shaman	SMEs, harpooner	Reports, standard pricing	Proposal prepared
Capture	13	Present the proposal	14 days	Shaman	Harpooner	Proposal, script	Presentation completed
	14	Whale decision making	21 days	Harpooner	Shaman, SMEs	Continual contact	Visits completed

	#	Task	Duration			Legal	Final agreement
	15	Negotiations on price, terms, and legal	14 days	Harpooner	Shaman, SMEs	Legal	Final agreement
	16	Vendor of Choice	7 days	Harpooner	Shaman, Chief	Contract	Purchase order issued
	17	Notification of order and capacity planning	1 day	Harpooner	Village	Scheduling and manpower assignments	Notification with details sent out
	18	Internal kickoff (review)	5 days	Project manager	All	P.O., discovery info	Handoff
Sew	19	External kickoff (with whale)	5 days	Project manager	Account manager	Contract	Conference call completed
	20	Hardware configuration	Concurrent	Project manager	Project team	Hardware	Hardware setup
	21	Conversion files and file layouts received	21 days	Project manager	Project team	Conversion documents	Information received

Well, they can't necessarily control, but they must understand and report. Over time, you learn what is a normal, or standard, response time for your key prospects in your markets. What's important, therefore, is not the time cycle itself but how it can give you insight into the whale's behavior. If you are accustomed to hearing something about your proposal within 21 days after you've submitted it, your antenna should go sky high if you hear nothing from the whale for 30 days. It's a signal of something—you don't know what, but it is a signal. It should spur your team to action—make a call, pay a visit, conduct an inquiry—to find out what's going on and assess what it means to you.

Motion versus Movement

Think of a typical sales meeting devoted to "the big deal." We hear the voices of the meeting participants:

> Sales Manager: Five weeks ago, you told me that this was a "darn near done deal" after you submitted the proposal.
> Sales Rep: It was. . .
> Sales Manager: Four weeks ago, you said that the prospect was reviewing the proposal and they were ready to sign.
> Sales Rep: They were. . .
> Sales Manager: Three weeks ago, you said that they had a few "standard questions" for us and that it would be signed by the end of the week.
> Sales Rep: That's what happened. . .
> Sales Manager: Two weeks ago, you said that they wanted to visit us again and you thought that it was a good thing because it meant that they must be really interested. Then last week

they asked us to rescope a portion of the proposal. Now this week you want to go back out there—is this deal done or not?

Sales Rep: Boss, we are so close I can feel it—we'll have it closed this week!

Sales Manager: You said that five weeks ago!

These conversations are the norm, not the exception. The focus is on the back-and-forth communication between the harpooner and the whale. If you review the discussion, you can see that your company and the whale did a lot of work over five weeks' time—meetings, meetings, e-mails, phone calls, visits, preparation, and exchanges of documents. But, after five weeks, are you any closer to a deal? No! You are still at "proposal"—the same place you started five weeks back.

We call this the "motion trap." Discussing the back-and-forth communication simply reflects motion inside of a step in an articulated sales process. It may be important to understand, but it gets you nowhere. You have to separate out "motion" from "movement."

Six Criteria for Every Sales Step

- *Owner*
- *Roles and responsibilities*
- *Resources required*
- *Subprocess*
- *Metrics/success criteria*
- *Timeline*

Once you have defined your steps and the six criteria of every step, you should be looking weekly at every opportunity in your pipeline to determine where it is and how long it has been there. Anecdotal discussions of communication trap you in motion discussions. What's important is the progress of the current step and what it will take to get to the next step. The sales cycle to whales is often long. If you analyze it only at the end, the final yes or no of the deal, your company buries important information that you could translate into priceless knowledge. You miss learning which parts of your sales process should be improved. Or which components give you the greatest leverage. Most important, you miss learning which whales should be retired to Baja, taken out of the current sales pipeline, because they are not going to close. The sales process and the timeline by step will tell you when a deal is dead but has not yet been declared and buried.

Sales Meeting Questions

1. *At which step is this whale in our sales process?*
2. *How long has it been there and when will it be moving on?*
3. *What action are we taking to move it to the next step?*
4. *Should this whale be taken out of our pipeline?*
5. *Which steps are consistently working and which steps are not?*
6. *How can we make our nonworking steps perform better?*

Watch carefully the time between sales process steps. If it stretches out beyond your expectations, you are most likely losing. And watch carefully the time between promises and delivery by your prospect. Whale-sized deals require lots of information and involvement on the part of the whale. In many of the sales steps, both you and the whale walk away with commitments made to each other. A whale that consistently misses commitment dates, doesn't return inquiries, and pushes back delivery dates demonstrates a fundamental lack of interest.

Motion is back-and-forth activity within a single step. Movement, in contrast, is completing a step and, subsequently, working on the next step in your process. Knowing and acting on the difference makes for whale-hunting success.

Use Your Map to Improve

Once you have mapped your whale-hunting process and completed an initial assessment of how much time you should allot for each step, you can use your new knowledge to improve your process, often in very significant ways.

Our client, Echo Supply, is a manufacturer of molded parts for the automotive industry. During the period of our engagement with them, they were building new business relationships in China. They intended to manufacture parts in China that would be delivered to a buyer in the United States.

After working with their sales process map, they discovered that the period of time to produce a prototype for a customer was too long because of the issues with language and culture between here and China. So they created a Chinese counterpart to quality and sourcing in China to mirror the U.S.-based engineering, sourcing, and quality team. Then they made investments in their own manufacturing plant in China to supplement their other manufacturing partners there. Now they have sourcing, quality, and engineering on both sides of the ocean. They also have their own manufacturing in China, as well as contract manufacturing in China.

Another of our clients, Ontario Systems, sells a complex product and service, which requires a long sales process and an even longer implementation process. We worked with their team to map the sales process throughout every step, including all steps of the implementation. An issue arose about the timing of their requirements analysis. In the past, completion of the requirements scope document (RSD) occurred at the beginning of the implementation of the new system. The scope decisions that were made during the sales process were less formal—although many were contractual—and the project management personnel both at Ontario Systems and within the customer company had not necessarily been involved in the definition of scope requirements.

The RSD is a complex process, requiring two to three days of consultation between customer representatives and a team from Ontario Systems. The sales team was concerned that requiring the RSD to be conducted presale would slow the sales process. Could they be guaranteed that the appropriate personnel resources would be available when they needed them? Would it be necessary to charge the prospective customer for this service? Would it take too long? Would the outcomes provide valuable information to Ontario's competitors? In short, how would they assess the relative merits and risks of making this kind of process change?

After testing the new model, the company accomplished several comprehensive requirements analyses presale, and defined a modified version of the RSD that can be accomplished more quickly and at less expense. In both cases, sales and operations collaborated to find solutions for the enterprise.

Share Your Map with the Whale

The harpooner is responsible to understand every whale's established buying process. Don't assume the potential customer will offer that information. Use information from your prospect to customize your sales map for this deal. Add all necessary steps of your own.

Then write down this customized sales process in a formal document and share it with the buyers' table. Seek agreement on this sales process from all relevant parties, first within your village and then from the whale. As basic as this may sound, many organizations fail to inform their prospect as to how the process should move forward. Everyone at the buyers' table and everyone on your boat should receive this document and be contacted to ensure that they concur with the steps and the time given to each step. Include clear and definite timelines. Of course, putting things in writing does not guarantee compliance. However, the gentle reminder of a written document, appropriately shared within both organizations, creates an implied sense of obligation. It also notifies the whale of your schedule for acceptance of the opportunity.

This practice helps you to determine whether the whale is serious, and can save you time and money in a futile hunt. Sometimes, a whale puts out feelers into the marketplace, giving signals that it is looking for a new vendor, when it is actually just testing the market. It may be trying to find out if its current arrangement is the best available, or a way of exerting pressure on its current vendor to lower prices or add services, with no intention of going to the trouble of actually making changes.

Don't play that game. Let the whale get its information elsewhere. You will be spending extensive time and money on the complex sale, so don't waste your assets on a deal that would be impossible to sign. Your assets are finite. Spending your time trying to land a whale you have no chance of actually harvesting prevents you from working a prospect that you could land.

Validate each step as you go along. In the Whale Hunters' Process, each significant movement is tracked, measured, and validated. Contact each person who initially received a copy of the sales process as you complete each step and begin the next step. If the process calls for your harpooner and an expert oarsman to visit the prospect's branch offices within the next two weeks to determine how the computer systems match up, complete the step on time. Then follow up with a report on the results of the visit and announce you are starting the next step and when that step is to be complete.

Quickly renegotiate any missed dates. Often a client will move back the timeline, saying, "I am not sure when we will get to the next step." A good harpooner will not let this go. Real questions have to be answered, such as: "Will the project still occur?" "Will your organization be rebidding this project?" "Have you narrowed the field, and how do we stand?" "What can we do to be helpful during the interim while you still have this need but no agreed-upon solution?"

If things begin going badly, with missed deadlines and no new schedule for getting back on track, you must be willing to take the must difficult step of all—walking away. The hardest thing a harpooner has to do is cut the line on a whale that is going to be impossible to land. A whale that will damage the boat, risk the crew, or become too heavy to tow back to shore is not a whale worth taking. Time kills all deals!

Complex sales can quickly go out of control, especially when you begin to think your relationship with the whale-sized prospect is assured. Suddenly the buyer can begin trying to purchase services faster than you can sell them. Other times the process can stall, and you realize a deal might not occur at all. Whether things begin moving too quickly or too slowly, you now have to face a series of challenges for the harpooners and village.

Never trust the fast yes. Nothing makes the harpooner happier than the prospect saying yes quickly. However, there are a number of risks associated with the fast yes.

Even when the prospect expresses willingness to sign a contract or letter of agreement, you must remain cautious. In the complex sale, when you are beginning what you hope to be a long and profitable relationship, the quick yes can lead to mistakes. It can prove to have come from someone who lacks the authority to sign. It can encourage bypassing important presale processes like credit checks. It can leave you with a disenfranchised operational team because there wasn't sufficient time for everyone to prepare for a whale-sized deal. It can result in the new customer having inaccurate expectations of what you offer and plan to supply. Further, the chances are extremely low that you will benefit from trying to enforce a quickly signed agreement or contract. You want to establish a good reputation within the marketplace and a profitable relationship with a large stable company. You aren't looking for legal action.

Create the Proposal

If everything goes well in your sales process, you will be invited to put a proposal in front of your whale. The proposal is another opportunity for you to differentiate your company and your services; it is also an opportunity to sink more time and money into a low-probability deal. Therefore, the first rule for a proposal is to be certain that you have completed all of the preliminary steps that tell you the whale is ready to move forward if your value proposition meets its needs.

A proposal has "legs." Once it is in writing, it will visit places you have never been as a salesperson. It will wind up on the desks of people who don't know you, or others who don't like you. For that reason, you can't take anything for granted. The nuanced conversations about minor capabilities in the mosaic of your service offering could be the most important features to a subject matter expert who was not included in earlier discussions. Here are some recommendations to create a winning proposal:

- *Create an executive summary.* This one-page document will have the most legs of all. The format is simple. What is the problem being addressed? What is the solution being proposed? How much will it cost? What is the timeline? What is the process to accomplish all items above? If it takes longer than one page to say what needs to be said, start over.
- *Include navigation tools.* Use page numbers, a table of contents, color-coding, and signposting of icons by section, indexes, and tabs to make it easy for all readers to find what they want.
- *Cull out your propaganda.* Watch out for the sales-y boilerplate, and eliminate as much as possible. If you can't tie it to the customer's benefits, leave it out.
- *Make the document benefits-rich.* Every feature should link to a benefit. What does the customer get specifically for each feature that is included? If you can't find a "top box" benefit for a feature, leave it out.
- *Include a call to action.* At the bottom of the executive summary and at the end of the pricing page, include a place for a sign-off from the client. This is part of the "trial close."
- *Give them choices.* No proposal should have only one take-it-or-leave-it price. Offer choices that clearly enumerate price/value relationships.

- *Define a timeline.* All proposals should have a duration for which the quote or price will be valid.
- *Read and revise the completed document.* Often a proposal is a team effort, with a customer-specific cover letter, executive summary, a scope of work, and a pricing page, with the other components cobbled together from existing materials. Make sure that job is handled by a subject matter expert who is very detail-oriented and experienced in preparing proposals, and who will make sure that the final document will be cohesive—it should read as if written in one voice.
- *Present the proposal in person.* If the buyers' table will not invest time to hear you present, they may not be very serious about doing business with you. You may want to use a PowerPoint for the presentation, with a written packet to leave with each participant. Include extras for people who are not present.

Note: This is not the Magna Carta. Say only what needs to be said and no more. Brevity equals clarity and simplicity of understanding.

Harpooning with an RFP

What do you do when an ideal whale keeps its distance by using an RFP/RFQ process to select a vendor or partner for a large opportunity?

Regulated industries, government agencies, and many others handle purchasing for complex projects through the request for proposals/request for qualifications. They use these methods to purchase IT, research, consulting, logistics, training, manufacturing, assembly, printing—any large product or service that you can imagine.

Whale hunters hate to wield an RFP response instead of their own harpoon. Here's why:

- *Low yield:* Three percent is the national average for closing an RFP deal. Of all the RFPs submitted, only 3 percent result in new business for the responding firm. The odds against winning are ridiculous.
- *Deficit-based:* RFPs don't intend to highlight the strengths of your firm. They are designed to protect the whale from making a bad decision, rather than to help the whale make "the best" decision.
- *Price sensitivity:* RFP processes force information into a matrix that often makes price the main differentiating characteristic.
- *Market intelligence risk:* A whale may use the RFP process to leverage pricing and performance concessions from the current provider with no intention of changing. In that case, all of your work makes the whale's life easier but provides no opportunity for you. In dishonorable cases, the whale might provide your solutions and prices to internal or external competitors for the business.

Despite these risks, a great deal of business is awarded through the RFP process—business that you may want from whales that are ideal for you. So how do you increase your odds of winning greater than a measly 3 percent? Sure, the old advice is true, if you write the RFQ or RFP format, you have a better chance—everybody gets that. But that's rarely the case. Now what else?

Ten Ways to Win through Whale Hunting Principles

1. *Play only to win (aka "just say no").* Answering every RFP that crosses your desk guarantees you a 3 percent or less close ratio.

Define a strategy that eliminates more than 75 percent of the RFPs that you look at before you type a single answer to a single RFP requirement. Refusing most of the RFPs will save you money, time, and frustration.

2. *Play by the rules.* Every detail of the submission process needs to follow directions explicitly. There are some simple do's and don'ts:

   - Do guide the readers through your response to their requirements.
   - Do follow the RFP's outline for how to respond.
   - Do provide the requisite references to key points in the RFP.
   - Don't exceed the page requirements.
   - Don't reduce the font size.
   - Don't submit it late.
   - Don't skip any question or section.

3. *Develop advocates (we call them "ravens.")* In the Inuit culture, a raven is an advocate of the shaman. In modern whale hunting, a raven is an advocate of yours who is an insider on this deal or who has access to insiders. Using the RFP process as an entry point with a new whale predicts low odds of winning. You have no access to information, no understanding of the discrete buying issues and politics, and no champion. RFPs from whales you know and with which you have some relationship give you better odds. But if you receive an interesting RFP from a whale with which you have not done business, use the RFP as a reason to meet, even by telephone, to review the RFP and ask for more information. If you can't find or develop a raven, do not respond.

4. *Use the system.* Once you've decided to pursue the RFP, use every opportunity that the whale provides to educate you. Attend all information sessions. Track responses to questions posed by other

bidders. Typically, there is an early time period during which the whale will freely exchange information with you. Take advantage of this opportunity early and often. Call. Ask questions. Seek guidance. This practice will prepare you for future RFP responses, even if you choose not to respond to this one.

5. *Compete on price—alpha.* The process favors low pricing; so, if you are high-priced, you probably will not win. Period. Forget whether that is fair or right. Here is the issue to consider: Every company we know has a pricing sweet spot—a place where they have developed some efficiencies that allow them to be more cost-effective than others. You have to determine whether the pricing being examined falls within your sweet spot. If it doesn't, pass. Price is a qualifier. If you can't qualify, don't play.

6. *Compete on price—beta.* Several of our clients have been very successful in the pricing game because they understood their whales very well. They knew that their whale would evaluate the base quote against all other quotes and compare the bidders on that basis alone. Change orders, secondary fees, and other charges would not be given much weight because they could not be truly anticipated in the contract as to frequency and volume. One client's successful strategy was to win the contract at cost and win the margin on secondary fees. If you know your whale, you can win.

7. *Promise safety—reduce risk.* The people who represent your whale have one primary goal in mind: Don't make a mistake. When you are a small or midsize business responding to a whale's RFP, your most important message is "no risk." Your innovation, your new ideas, your novel practices—all of these pale in comparison to your experiential track record. Make the safety case first.

8. *Enlist expertise.* As you pursue a strategic big opportunity, seek expert help. Maybe your annual revenues are $10 million and you are bidding on an RFP for $100 million of work. It's a transformational opportunity for your company. Once you've decided that this RFP is looking for expertise that you can provide at a price that is attractive to you, invest in a "capture team," whose members have expertise in completing RFPs for this whale and in doing business with the whale.

9. *Tell your story.* RFPs are laden with jargon and "business speak," and they beguile you to respond in kind. Resist that temptation! Our advice is to write your RFQ responses as a narrative, with a target audience of an eighth-grade reader, not an industry insider. Your goal is clarity and consistency; it is not to talk down to your reader. Simple clarity expressed in ordinary language will give the whale confidence in your understanding of the work for which you are bidding

10. *Evoke the reader.* Even if you're submitting an RFP to a government agency or a multinational corporation, *real people* are charged to read and respond to your proposal. Try to put yourself in that position. Their *first goal* is to reject your proposal on any technical ground. Their *second goal* is to find an easy win. Their *third goal* is to satisfy individual specific interests. RFPs are often read by a number of people who skim the answers, looking for the parts that are interesting to them. So if you want to leverage your response and emphasize your value, get used to repeating yourself, strategically. To emphasize what you bring, express your value proposition wherever you can.

Fundamentally, whales use the RFP process to determine minimal qualifications, not to select the ultimate providers. The RFP process is not where or when you sell your competitive advantages. Sell your minimal qualifications with the goal of being selected as a finalist to present to the selection group.

The capture phase of whale hunting looms long and tedious. In your early hunts, you will have a great deal of work to do in preparation. Setting up your discovery/disclosure chart; identifying all the important steps in a sales process for whales; and defining roles, responsibilities, and time frames may seem like far too much work. And perhaps it is too much work if you want to do business as usual. But if whale hunting is your goal, you are not setting out to land a single whale. Rather, you are building capacity in your company to hunt and harvest a steady diet of whales. The work of the capture builds provides transparency, learning, and commitment across your functional areas. It makes you better. When you do it well, you are ready to sew the whale's mouth shut—that is, close the deal.

Capture the Whale Action Items

- *Define and refine all steps in your process of progressive discovery/ progressive disclosure to ensure that your boat learns what it needs to know at every step of the process.*
- *Map your whale hunting process, communicate it to everyone in your village, and test and refine your timetables so that you will know when to stop a hunt.*
- *Design and implement processes for creating proposals to whales that will increase the likelihood that the whale will say yes.*

Please visit www.thewhalehunters.com to download the sales process tools introduced in this chapter.

8

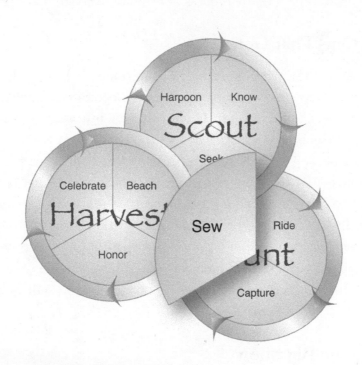

Sew the Mouth Shut

AFTER THE INUIT HUNTERS HARPOONED their whale and rode it until it ceased fighting, one dangerous maneuver remained before the hunters could start for shore. In the rugged conditions of the open ocean, a dead whale on the surface of the water wouldn't last long. If the whale's mouth were allowed to gape open, water would lap in, filling the body cavity. Eventually, the prize that the hunters worked so hard to capture would disappear into the ocean, sinking beneath the waves.

One of the hunters must slip out of the boat into the freezing water and, using sealskin line, tie the mouth shut to keep the water out. It is one of the first techniques the Inuit use to protect their whale during the lengthy process of bringing it to shore.

The One That Got Away

Have you ever had a verbal commitment to buy that fell through? Have you ever sent a mutually negotiated contract that your prospect failed to sign? Have you ever lost a deal even after you had a signed contract? Of course you have.

This phase of whale hunting is the most dangerous phase for your village. By the time you reach the point of contract negotiations, you have invested a great amount of resources to land this whale. In addition to the valuable time of the people on the boat, you may have created costly prototypes, spent money on travel and materials, and entertained members of the buyers' table.

In this chapter, we offer a series of tactics that will help you take your deal to a firm close.

Stage the Big Show

A critical step in the whale hunt is the day when the whale pays you a visit. By this time, you have carefully navigated the stages of qualifying, first meeting, and proof of concept sharing—progressively discovering key information about the whale and disclosing pertinent details about yourselves. You know who is at the buyers' table and you've populated your boat with appropriate subject matter experts. Through the process, you have gained a clearer understanding of the whale's needs, and generated specific ideas for how your company will meet those needs.

You are getting clear buy signals from the right people on the prospect's team. Yet you can sense that the whale still feels that nagging fear—fear of change, conflict, mistakes, or work, all of these. Simply put, working with your company or implementing your solution looks scary—too risky, too untested—from the whale's perspective. If you haven't invited members of the buyers' table to visit you at your facility, now is the time.

When company's coming, do everything you can to mitigate their fear. Prepare with precision, implement flawlessly, and follow up with speed and care. During and after the visit, take every opportunity to press into service the four fear busters: people, process, technology, and experience. Anything less could worsen the whale's fear and send it comfortably back to that same old way of doing business, which you are trying to crack.

We call this visit the "big show." Implementing your version of the big show can have powerful outcomes in closing your whale hunting deals.

Prepare with Precision

When a whale visits your company headquarters, all of your employees should be prepared to orchestrate the big show. To prepare those who will be in face-to-face conversations, you need to gain as much knowledge as possible about the relevant existing processes within the whale and share that knowledge with the presenters. You will want your employees to be able to express their roles so as to demonstrate the parallels between the current and proposed conditions for your prospect. That understanding will help the buyers to feel comfort and safety. In addition to preparing the employees actually involved in meetings, consider also the power of the visit when everyone at your location knows the prospect, knows the date and time of the visit, and understands the importance of the big show to the company's success and, therefore, to their personal success. To ensure that understanding, take the following steps:

1. Announce the whale's visit to all employees well ahead of the visit.
2. Send a dossier to everyone who will be in touch with the whale.
3. Prepare and distribute two versions of the agenda, planned in 15-minute increments:
   - A detailed backstage agenda for participants from your organization
   - A front-stage agenda for all whale invitees
4. Pair your subject matter experts with whale counterparts so the pairs may deal with specific issues and agenda items.
5. Assign and communicate clear roles and responsibilities to all participants.
6. Remind all employees the day before to dress appropriately and to clean and organize their work areas.
7. Check and double-check infrastructure—lighting, technology, parking, internal operations, seating arrangements, name badges—to ensure working order on the day of the visit.
8. Demonstrate visual indicators of control and performance: display customer testimonials on mobile whiteboards, illustrate

department performance with strategically placed charts and graphs, position computer screens and dashboards so that the visitors can see them.
9. Rehearse, rehearse, rehearse.

Implement Flawlessly

From the receptionist's smile to the Q&A session, from the software demonstration to the very last handshake, let every message say to the whale, "We will perform this deal with excellence."

1. Greet the invitees by name; welcome them with a big sign in your reception area.
2. Follow the agenda and seating chart.
3. Provide appropriate refreshments throughout the day, ensuring that the workspace is set and reset to be continually fresh and welcoming.
4. Prepare your presenters for two important functions: to gather information and to demonstrate knowledge and capability.
5. If you are presenting:
   - Make clear your understanding of the whale's needs.
   - Highlight your tools, processes, systems, and other methods that mitigate fears.
   - Involve other subject matter experts at appropriate moments to reveal their expertise.
6. Answer the whale's questions. Acknowledge those you can't answer and commit to answering them promptly.
7. Thank the whale for visiting, and agree upon next steps together.

Follow Up Quickly and Thoughtfully

Waste no time in reinforcing the first two acts in the big show.

1. Answer all pending questions.
2. Follow through on all commitments.
3. Thank and provide feedback to all internal participants.
4. Discuss and document lessons learned, for continuous improvement.
5. Tell everyone the outcomes as soon as you know.

Our client, Langham Logistics, honed the big show process to great effect. They became experts at giving prospective customers a tour of their office, shipping, and warehouse facilities, involving key employees from all facets of their business.

The following are excerpts from the process they developed.

1. They clarified for all employees the "sensations that we hope our visitors will feel from our tour." These include:
   - Langham takes its business seriously.
   - Langham is thoughtful in the way that it conducts its business.
   - Langham is friendly in how it treats its people, carriers, and clients.
   - Langham is confident in its ability to do a good job because its people and processes are capable.
2. Next they created an overview of the benefits they wanted to demonstrate and the methods by which they would demonstrate those benefits. Table 8.1 gives a sample.

Finally, Langham developed a detailed outline of their tour, including each stop along the way, the person who would be speaking

Table 8.1 Langham Benefits Overview

Benefit	Feature	How We Achieve
Ease of use	One-stop	Experience
	Customize	People
	Friendly people	Clients
	Technology	Applications
Security/fear—uncertainty and doubt	Cost optimization	Process
	Reputation/integrity	ISO certification
	Fewer errors/smarter methods	Langham way
	Regulation compliance	Technology
		Online reporting
Ego	Affiliation	PKS
	WBE	EDI
	People like us	TransSoft

at that stop, and the props that would be visible. Here is an example of one of the stops on their tour:

Stop 2: Pivot Desk—Betty

- Greatest level of experience—this is where we started.
  - Visibility, trackability, traceability
  - Phone or web
- Creativity
  - Midroute corrections
  - Optimization/intelligent choices

- Expedited
  - Problems are us
- Shipment tracking
  - Available satellite tracking
  - Active status notification
  - Traceability
  - Transit times
  - Appointment times
- Reporting
  - Standardized information
  - Online access
  - Customized
- Air freight

> **Prop 1: Enterprise System**
>
> - Note Taking
> - Example 1
> - Example 2
>
> **Prop 2: Company Profile**
>
> **Prop 3: Customized Reports**
>
> - Status Update

Every stop on the Langham tour has been crafted at this level of detail. The company is able to highlight its people, processes, technology, and experience in deep and believable ways because of their preparation and rehearsal.

Another of our clients, SGI Inc. crafts the big show based on the whale's fears, how the tour will allay those fears, and the total impression SGI intends to leave with the whale. Here's an example of how SGI communicates these key points to their internal team.

[Customer's] primary fears are:

1. The cost of change will outweigh the benefits of moving.
2. There will be errors made during transition that will damage his/her reputation and put his/her internal customers through unnecessary turmoil.
3. It will require too much effort for his/her team to make the change.

Experiences we want [the customer] to have:

1. The depth of our executive team.
2. How well we manage the client relationship.
3. See actual fulfillment operations of similar profile.
4. How we manage IT development from beginning to end.

We want [the customer] to leave here with the feeling that:

1. His/her desire for our technology solutions is reinforced.
2. Our approach to planning and management of accounts and transitions will reduce any potential errors and reduce risk of change.
3. Our transition management experience will reduce risk and the amount of time his/her team will need to invest during transition.
4. We handle work exactly like his/hers and are more than big enough to handle the work.
5. We have an account management structure and team that will deliver a high level of service.
6. We are a progressive company investing in new technologies all the time, and this will help control his/her costs.

These key points are reinforced in the day's agenda and the script for each stop on the tour. Every participant knows the purpose and the point.

The Whale Hunters have been privileged to work for a number of clients who have honed their big show for prospects. These companies have a near 100 percent close rate on whale-sized deals when they are able to host the prospect's buying team at their facility.

Other clients who had never practiced the big show found it to be a big step forward in their sales process development when they began using it.

You will find amazing by-products from staging the big show. The first time you invite a major prospect to visit your home base, you and core team members will begin to look at your place of business with fresh eyes. Is your reception area welcoming? Do your departments appear well organized? Is it an appealing workplace? Are your meeting spaces clean and inviting? Do people take pride in maintaining their work areas? Often, in a fast-growing company, the answers to all of these questions is no! The first time you host an important visit, you may have to scramble to put the place in order. Maybe you'll want to paint walls and order in some live plants. You will meet a certain amount of resistance from people who see this as a phony ploy, a distraction from their "real work."

Yet we have found that the big show builds pride among your staff, and motivates many people to maintain a "visitor-ready" workplace. And here we must reiterate an important point: This process of "putting your best foot forward" is more than a big show for your prospects. It calls attention to many things that can be improved in your workplace; it gives your leadership team a new perspective, and instills in them a new pride and a more externally focused way of looking at all sorts of things. Therefore, it has the effect of making you better, not just making you look good.

More Credibility Builders

When you are trying to close a deal that is much larger than your average deal, you may have to increase your capacity in a variety of ways—adding personnel; leasing, buying, or building additional space; adding new locations or adding new equipment. You will need to demonstrate to the whale that you have concrete, viable plans for how to accomplish all of the new capacity. Here are some examples from our own experience:

- Our client, Echo Supply, located in Indianapolis, sold a huge deal to a company in China. As part of sewing the mouth shut, they illustrated a ramping plan inside of their plant, including the types of equipment they would buy, how it would be used, and what the additional capacity would provide in terms of manufacturing capacity. Their illustration included a detailed install, "burn-in," certification, and first-run plan.

- Another of our clients, Midwest Mole, won a huge subcontract to dig a trenchless tunnel as part of the building of a new mid-field terminal at the Indianapolis airport. The 2016-foot tunnel for utility service had to go under an existing runway and two taxiways, at a depth of 22 feet underground, and would take four months to drill. To win the bid, Midwest Mole had to show that they had sourced the correct equipment and technology (a new 207,000-pound machine), had identified a subject matter expert engineer to manage the project, and had run similar projects. They provided demonstrations of how they would use the equipment to dig this amazing tunnel.

- When Tom Searcy was running Transcom, selling call center business in Europe, his team built architectural models of the facilities that would be built for their new customers, including technology schematics of the integrated call center environments, Pan-European and multilingual. They showed their prospects the training manuals, ramping schedules, CVs of current candidates being interviewed, even flight schedules showing the ease of reaching the locations, and relatively inexpensive cost.

- Machine Specialties, also a client, was involved in a very detailed bid to become a prime contractor to the U.S. Air Force for the manufacture and delivery of landing-gear parts. In their proposal, they called attention to all of the investments they had made to prepare for this contract, even though the contract award was 18 months away. Significantly, they created a complete logistics plan, specific to the location of warehouses that they would build when they were awarded a contract.

These strategies are not just good ideas to earn the trust of the whale. They are good business practices to ensure that when you land the whale, you will be able to harvest it in exactly the way you proposed and to the specifications you promised.

Anticipate the Spoilers

In the business world, it is also important that you do everything possible to protect your deal. Whenever you are a small business doing business with a much larger company, you are always at risk, even after a contract has been signed. Be vigilant in your follow-up and diligent in your communications.

Three different spoilers can steal your deal after the prospect has given a verbal commitment.

The first spoiler to watch for is the incumbent provider—the provider you believe you have replaced. Like the ocean that can reclaim the whale, the minute the previous provider learns of its loss it will begin an all-out effort to regain any portion of the business. Otherwise poor-performing competitors will step up with extraordinary concessions or promises to get another chance with a customer.

Getting buy-in from the specialist buyers on your unique ability to change the business is particularly important when battling the incumbent provider. Frequently, the field people within the prospect whale aren't excited about all the work necessary to make changes. They can work to support the old provider, unless you have convinced them of the value of doing business with you.

The second spoiler resides inside the whale. It may be someone at or near the buyers' table who was insufficiently convinced during the sales process. Perhaps the opinion of a neglected midlevel manager was disregarded by the executive decision maker. This internal spoiler can also be an entire department, one that is starving for resources and threatened by an outsourced solution.

The third spoilers will descend en masse the minute you believe you have a deal secured and let down your guard. They are all your competitors in the marketplace. They will step in at any point that you leave an opening. You must assume that however certain your harpooners are that your negotiations and proposals have been kept private, they may well be wrong. Discussing the details of a progressing deal is human nature. So your competitors will immediately move in using inside intelligence to try to steal away your deal. Like the sharks and other sea predators that try to steal a meal from a captured whale, your competitors will come to feed.

In the Whale Hunters' Process, sewing the mouth shut is the phase when you get ahead of the spoilers. This process starts by anticipating all negative possibilities and designing a defense for each one.

Before anyone starts celebrating a successful sale, get your entire team together to map out a defense. Consider every possible way a spoiler could get a foot in the door. List the possibilities and design a defense for each one. Go down the spoiler categories. What do you know about the incumbent provider? Which of the technical buyers will they contact to try to get their foot back in the door?

Ask yourself which of the specialist buyers appear most concerned about your taking over this deal? Which of these buyers appeared the least impressed with your approach? Which have been the most noncommittal? Has their silence masked the fact that they are your adversary?

In both these cases you need to respond to each of these question marks by going to each of the problem buyers, reinforcing your case for change and your unique ability to effect it.

In the case of your competitors, take a close look at each one. Which of these adversaries would be most likely to step in to try to head off your deal? Which of your competitive advances would these competitors try to dispute? Take these competitors and issues head-on. Try to blunt the arguments before they are even made.

As part of this step, contact all the specialist buyers and field people who were important to your efforts and make sure all their questions have been answered. Keep in close communication with them. Besides protecting your deal, this step can also seal your relationships for the future. Many buyers will expect you to forget about them after agreements are signed. Take this opportunity to prove them wrong.

It is important that you act as though any signed agreements or contracts aren't sufficient to protect your deal. Legally enforcing these types of agreements is seldom worth it. Legal steps are time-consuming and expensive and usually mean that you will never again be able to work with this whale. Instead of relying on legalities, rely on an effective plan.

Initiate some direct business activity as quickly as possible. Even if regular activities under the contract aren't set to start for awhile, find some reason to do business now. Prove yourself, even in small matters.

Find a way to get some money to change hands. Provide a service or product, and send out an invoice as soon as possible. Paying that first invoice changes the relationship—whereas you used to be a sales organization, now you are a vendor or supplier. On your end, the company that used to be a prospect has become a customer. Once they have paid you for a product or service, it cements a bond between your company and the whale and adds immediacy to the relationship.

Put Your Chief in the Boat

Until now, we have talked about the harpooner, the shaman, and a team of subject matter experts making up your boat. But at the latter stages of a hunt you may find a new person in your boat—the chief. The CEO of a small to midsize company may feel compelled to participate in the sale of a big deal. Or the team may decide that it's judicious to involve the chief. Of course, you may be the chief of your village, in which case this passage is even more important for you to read and understand.

The chief in any village is the source of ultimate decision making. In successful companies, the chief's power derives from wisdom, fierceness in the face of adversity, accumulated knowledge of what works and what doesn't, and the ability to surpass the competition. CEOs are generally nervous when their company is hunting whales, and can only calm those nerves by getting involved.

As a valuable asset, your top officer needs to be used judiciously, appropriately, and regularly. It is not just a matter of respect to choose the proper pursuit for your chief; it is also an issue of allocating resources. Engage chiefs in opportunities that are too small, and they will lose interest in the prospect and question the pursuit's legitimacy. Engage them in dialog with junior persons, and you risk implying to the prospect that you are too small a firm, or are micro-managed to the point of ineffectiveness. Engage them too early, and the piece of business will appear to have more weight to the future of your firm than you want to relay to your prospect.

Your chief should be meeting with the most important economic driver in your prospect's firm. Often the person responsible for finance, operations, marketing, or sales also meets this criterion. However, title is not the deciding factor. Buying power and authority of the prospect's executive are most important. Seek the person ultimately responsible for the whale's strategy decisions. This person and your chief share ultimate accountability for the project; therefore, a partnership makes sense.

Get your chief involved at the right time—on schedule and on purpose. Too early or too late can both bring about problems. As you develop and refine your Whale Hunters' Process, you will increase your understanding of the important touchpoints where the chief should be involved in the sale, and only with the proper signals from the whale.

The few meetings in which the chief is included have real sales power, if managed properly. As the leaders of their villages, CEOs can demonstrate pride in the organization and faith in their ability to deliver on promises. They can add the power of position by making personal commitments to the potential client. And your chief can share insight, creativity, and institutional memory to add value to the client.

Pride and faith in the organization are crucial to the sales process. Without strong internal belief from the top down, it will be impossible for the whale to share in that belief and make a positive decision about your company.

The chief should visibly demonstrate a personal commitment to the whale. This commitment can be in the form of a promise of follow-up calls, involvement in installation or start-up, or other tangible proofs of ongoing participation. Be absolutely certain that you document these commitments, then assist your chief in delivering on them. Your chief can help a client avoid missteps, approach problems from a different perspective, and think strategically about potential issues.

In contrast, leave the chief at home during price negotiations. The chief's role is to amplify the high value of your service offering, not to negotiate what the whale will pay. Involving the CEO here weakens your team and guarantees future difficulties in client management. The chief's role in setting price is behind the scenes, not in front of the prospect. Price decisions need to be made before or after meeting with the whale, with the chief demonstrating personal commitment by relaying the internal decisions to the whale.

But despite these considerations, using your chief regularly is a good idea. The CEO should not be the boat member of first choice or last resort, but the role and timing of involvement should be determined very early in the process of a hunt. Sporadically involving the chief demonstrates to prospects a clear lack of integration with the team, whereas predictable, scheduled inclusion eases the whale's anxiety. It's also instrumental in organizational understanding of the whale hunting process, the life cycle of the sale, and the need for a full boat for large pursuits.

A team functions well through repeated drills. You can't just rehearse looking like a team; you must work at it. Therefore, your chief needs a predictable and repeated role in the whale hunting process so that the organization will improve its ability to hunt together. The chief needs to be involved in preparation and rehearsal and to understand his or her specific role, just like all other members of the boat.

If your chief has been the de facto shaman and chief harpooner, it will be all the more important to embrace a team-based whale hunting process. Using CEOs judiciously as members of the boat reminds them that whale hunting is important, it takes time and money, and it involves a lot of people—and the returns on that investment are extraordinary.

Manage the Contracts

When you are at the point of completing a contract with a whale, your smaller company enters a new realm of vulnerability. Relationships that your shaman and harpooner have built with the members of the buyers' table give way to new people in the deal on both sides of the table. Your legal team, their legal team. Your financial people, their financial people. This is a time when your team can lose the deal that you thought was done. It is also a time when your company can prevail through superior understanding of your position relative to the whale (smaller), superior maneuverability than the whale (more flexible), and superior teamwork (easier communications).

If you typically sell smaller deals to smaller customers, your contract language may be accepted without much question and your terms agreed to without challenge. The whale customer, however, typically has an energetic and aggressive legal team protecting its interests throughout the contract negotiation process.

As you do business with whales, track the progress of your contracts. If you have clauses and requirements that are routinely rejected by the whale, change them to be more compatible. It is in your best interests to get the contract signed as soon as possible, with as few hitches as possible. Make it easy for the whale to do business with you. We are not advocating that you cave in on important features of what you have sold and what you will deliver, only that you rid your contracts of language that whales will not approve and that, ultimately, will be unenforceable.

Share of Mind, Share of Calendar

Typically, some period of time elapses between when you close the deal and when your company begins its delivery to the whale. The length of this time period varies widely by industry and by the product or service that you provide. In professional services, the delivery may be set to begin within a matter of a few weeks. In parts manufacturing, the delivery may not begin for months. We have worked with clients for whom the time frame between contract signing and delivery is as long as 18 months. The longer the time between closing the deal and delivering what you promised, the more vulnerable you become.

So you need to use this lag time deliberately, strategically, and imaginatively, to ensure that your company preserves the full measure of the deal. Typically, your company will undertake a great deal of preparation for the upcoming delivery. But if you do not share this activity with your new customer, they will be unaware of the quality of your preparation or its significance within your company.

Share-of-Mind Tactics

- *Formalize the handoff from your sales team to your delivery team.*
- *Create good reasons to meet with counterparts.*
- *Introduce and follow relationship management strategy.*
- *Commit delivery dates to both calendars.*
- *Communicate on a regular, predictable basis.*
- *Announce the deal publicly.*

The handoff from the sales team to the delivery or implementation team offers great opportunities to solidify your deal. Engage the subject matter experts from your boat in follow-up conversations with their counterparts from the buyers' table. Instruct them to ask who are the key people with whom their departments will be working as the contract is fulfilled. Invite key people to visit your place of business. Send people to visit the whale. Consider implementing a weekly or biweekly email or newsletter recording progress toward the start date.

Seek permission from your new customer to send a press release announcing your deal. Make it visible in trade publications. In every possible way, promote it as a "done deal." At the same time, do not lose sight of your vulnerability until the whale has committed considerable resources toward moving the delivery schedule forward.

When Whale Hunting Fails

This seems like an appropriate place to discuss the inevitable failures of a whale hunt. People ask us, "Have you ever had an occasion when whale hunting was not successful?" The answer, of course, is yes.

Just as the Inuit did not land a whale on every hunt, so modern businesses will experience at least an occasional failure. Whale hunting is a growth strategy that requires the coordination of many interdependent elements. If any one element is missing or not working well, the probability of failure increases. These examples illustrate reasons for a failed hunt or a failed hunting process:

- *The wrong whale*: The first phase in the whale hunting model is "know the whale"—define the odds-in-your-favor whale to hunt and harvest. One of our clients identified that their best whales would be of a size between $500,000 and $1,500,000 in first-year annual revenue. They spotted a whale prospect, launched a boat, and discovered that the opportunity was actually $5 million. They were ecstatic—what a great whale opportunity for growth for their company! However, the process for identifying their perfect whale had been rigorous and accurate; they were really best able to serve a whale no larger than $1.5 million. Entrepreneurial enthusiasm caused them to violate their own target filter parameters. This whale almost killed them, taking almost 15 months before they could "digest it" and start making money. Whale hunting works. Apply the system and you will land whales. Just remember to get only the whales you want.
- *No chief on the boat:* We hear many CEOs complain, "Look at our client list; it seems that I have to bring in all the big accounts. Why can't my salespeople bring in big accounts?" The fact is that whales demand that the CEO be involved in the relationship for a whale-sized opportunity. The whale knows it represents a big opportunity and that the work will demand a high level of resources and attention from your company. It wants to look

the chief in the eye during the sales process to feel comfortable. Furthermore, almost every new whale that you land will significantly change your company. You will add new processes, equipment, personnel, technology, or some other enterprise-changing element to your company to support the whale. The chief has to be a part of the whale hunt to envision and implement these changes. In our experience, when the CEO of a small to midsize business that is whale hunting does not participate actively and in the appropriate role during the hunt, that company's whale-hunting activity does not produce the outcomes the executive team expected.

- *No scout:* When companies are small, salespeople are expected to perform all nine phases of the sales process themselves—what we call scouting, hunting, and harvesting functions. As a company grows, it often segments sales activities into "hunters" and "farmers," which means that hunters both scout and hunt, and farmers both hunt and harvest. But when a company chooses to whale hunt, we believe that the three core areas of scouting, hunting, and harvesting are unique, each requiring dedicated personnel, tools, and processes to be effective.

  One company we worked with stuck to the hunter/farmer model, preferring not to invest in scouting resources. As a result, the hunters quickly reached their capacity for whale hunting, and there was little capacity to grow without hiring additional hunters. The capacity threshold is expensive. This company hunts whales; however, its growth is slower than it could be if it allocated the resources to the process. In the end, this strategy is pennywise and pound-foolish.

- *No boat:* "Seven people on one side of the table and me on the other: it felt less like a sales call and more like a firing squad."

This we heard from a harpooner at a client company. We are helping that company implement a whale-hunting process. They have recognized that by sending one sale person out to whale-sized opportunities they were scaring their whales. Whales learn from harpooners why they should work with your firm. However, to make them feel safe and willing to work with you, they need to understand what and how. Your boat—the subject matter experts in your company who speak at a peer-to-peer level with their counterparts in the whale—best provides this information.

Your investment in training and using the right number of operationally knowledgeable people will help you land whales and will give you an edge over competitors that are comparable in size to you.

- *No village:* "Our village pushes whales away from the shore when they happen to beach themselves." You may think we're exaggerating, but we have heard this lament from harpooners countless times. Companies that try to adopt whale hunting only as a sales strategy, rather than a culture change, find themselves with whales lining up in the bay and rotting on the shore.

In the world of whale hunting, a big new contract often includes ramp-up provisions that allow the whale to evaluate your key performance indicators in the early stages of the agreement, after which they will determine how quickly to implement the full contract. If your village is not completely engaged and committed, their performance will keep the whale on the shore, no matter how effective your sales process has been. Whale hunting is a way of life that allows everyone in the organization to win. It is a cultural change implemented in a process-based way. So, can whale hunting fail?

You bet. It can fail by being successful in landing the wrong whales; it can fail by partial implementation; and it can fail from a lack of organizational commitment in a variety of ways.

But as your company learns to avoid these pitfalls, your success is almost assured. To minimize failure, give rigorous attention to your preparation before the hunt and your analysis after the hunt.

This phase of whale hunting concludes the second major stage of the process—the hunt. From here, we move to the part we call harvest—the phases during which your company will beach, honor, and celebrate its whales.

Sew the Mouth Shut Action Items

- *Stage the big show to demonstrate your company's capacity.*
- *Anticipate the spoilers so that you can prevent their success.*
- *Use your chief judiciously in securing the deal.*
- *Get on the whale's calendar and stay on their minds, to keep them interested.*

Please visit www.thewhalehunters.com to download the sales process tools introduced in this chapter.

9

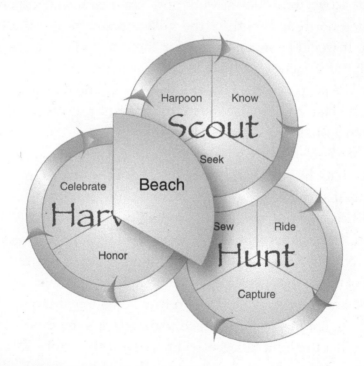

Beach the Whale

THE WHALE HAD STOPPED RESISTING, and the whale hunters had sewn its mouth shut. All that remained for the boat was to bring this 100,000-pound weight back to shore, at a place where their villagers could find them and assemble for the harvest.

They could not tow or tug the whale; it was far too large, heavy, and unwieldy. The boat, tackle, and crew weighed, all in, maybe 3,500 pounds. As in every other phase of the hunt, the whale hunters had to outthink, outmaneuver, and outsmart the whale, the elements, and other predators in the ocean. They learned to read the wind and the tides, working with the elements to reach the shoreline.

The scouts were back at work now, covering a wide expanse of shoreline north and south of the village, watching for the boat's return. It would be most unusual for the boat to land at the same place it was launched; far more likely to beach the whale at another point. The people on the boat and the people who remained in the village all had to know and understand how the process would work to beach a whale.

When a scout spotted the boat returning with a whale in tow, he would run to the village and alert everyone. They would rapidly pack all of their supplies—tools, buckets, pots and pans, sleds. Everyone would head for the anticipated landing spot on the shore—men, women, and children, the elderly, even the infirm if they were able. They took their dogs and their provisions. They had a huge task ahead of them, and there was no time to waste.

Imagine the collective strength it required to get the whale on the beach, not just near the beach. And imagine the short window of time that the Inuit villagers had to harvest the whale. The same wind and tides that helped them beach the whale could take it back out again.

As we have said before, the Inuit whale hunt was a sacred ritual. The Inuit believed that the whale was a gift from the gods to their people, and they treated the whale reverentially. In their earliest oral history, the whale and the land were one. The whale was sustenance—the whale was life itself.

There was a ceremony on the shore when the whale was beached. One of the highest-ranking people who had remained on land for the duration of the hunt welcomed the whale to the village and gave thanks for the whale.

Bringing a New Account On Board

Finally, you are landing the new account that your boat has pursued for some time. You have completed a formal process of identifying which unique product or service you have that would benefit this customer. Then you have identified and contacted the major buyers within the account. You communicated a clear message of the benefits you bring as a company. You were well received, and secured a letter of agreement. The contract was signed, and you are ready to begin delivering the products and services that you have sold.

In the past, this set of circumstances might have prompted a celebratory dinner for some of the primary employees involved in the deal, followed by the beginning of your customary internal start-up and launch process. Then, in fact, many of the peripheral people assigned to the sale might have been pulled off the account and assigned to the next deal in the sales pipeline.

But business as usual would be a mistake in the case of a new whale account. This is no time to relax your defenses. The business world is fraught with the empty hands of those who thought a deal was done only to find last-minute mistakes impeding progress.

In many of our engagements with clients, we encounter some animosity between sales and operations. The salespeople think that operations are too slow and insufficiently customer-oriented. The operations people think the salespeople are selling products and services the company is not fully prepared to deliver. Most of the people inside the company fear they cannot gear up or ramp up for a major new account.

It's not an irrational fear. If you are the chief or shaman responsible for bringing a huge new deal on board, you understand the need to have a certain amount of surety before you invest. Your staff, who will be responsible for delivering on the promises, may well worry that they will not have the people, the equipment, or the other resources they will need to do their best work. On the other hand, sometimes your people are just not ready to go to the next level of delivery.

Your company is highly vulnerable at this point in the sales process. You have a signed contract, and strategically we hope that you have at least one paid invoice. Nevertheless, the whale's go-forward decisions may be still in flux.

How soon will the whale commit to a start date? What percentage of the entire contract will be committed up front? What are the performance milestones, and what capabilities do you need to demonstrate to meet them? Our manufacturing clients, in particular, come face to face with big fears at this point in the process. The whale can scale down or slow down its buy at any moment, and you are almost powerless to prevent it. The antidote is to overdeliver, overachieve, and to ramp up faster than the whale can imagine.

To make that strategy work, you need all of your operations areas to be not only ready but also enthusiastically anticipating the new business.

The Village Is Too Busy for Whales!

Yogi Berra is famous for his many funny malapropisms. One of our favorites was, "That place is so busy, nobody goes there anymore!" Like the too-crowded restaurant, a village convinced that it can't hunt new whales because it is too busy with current responsibilities dooms itself to long-term difficulty and possible failure.

What are the symptoms of a village in overload mode? See if any of these sound familiar:

- "I'm so busy right now, I can't possibly put anything new on my plate."
- "You can never get Fred or Michelle to come to meetings, because they are too busy putting out fires."
- "Somebody has got to tell sales to slow down, or we will begin to lose people from overwork!"
- "If we are not careful, something is going to slip through the cracks, and then who are they going to blame?"
- "All we seem to do around here is meet and try to carve up the work in a different way so that it will get done. We really need a lot more people."

Capacity is a difficult balancing act for a company trying to grow fast. It is hard to anticipate properly the resources that you will need for new business while maintaining profitability and operational integrity. In essence, leadership is working with equations that have many variables, including new sales, current support, market conditions, customer satisfaction, and long-term goals. It makes your head swim to consider how many ways you can get this calculus wrong and how few ways you can get it right.

Yet a company too busy to take on new customers today is doomed to have no new customers tomorrow. A company must have eyes looking out for new opportunities as well as eyes looking down and doing the work. Without eyes looking both places, you will miss the whales—and perhaps the caribou, and the trout, and everything else it takes to keep your village alive.

Ideally, your company has created a filter to sort the work and consider it strategically. You've considered all the issues of resources, profitability, long-term product development, and other key metrics specific to your business. You've compared your opportunities against this filter and figured out which items should be shelved, delayed, or acted on. You've guarded the precious resource of your firm's time and have committed to take on only work that makes sense for you to do. Now is the time, if you haven't done so, to build a strategic plan that identifies the crunch points where you will need new capacity. Consider whether you should accomplish your additional capacity through technology, additional employees, realigned resources, outsource partners, or other creative options.

Whatever you decide, it will be important to keep your village on board and ready, even eager, to take on new whales.

Preparing the Village

Every employee in your company needs to be motivated and trained to harvest a new whale account successfully. To judge your readiness to beach a new whale, consider three key elements within your company:

- *Capacity*: Can you harvest a whale? You can't harvest until your village has the capacity to do so. We define a company's capacity not only by its internal assets and number of employees but also by its flexibility in organizing resources to harvest each whale.

You will increase your capacity to harvest as you increase your employees' ability to collaborate across divisional and departmental lines, and as you demonstrate that top management can and will provide sufficient resources, and organize those resources, to meet the harvest demands. A new whale brings tremendous new resources, as well as requiring new capacity. Therefore, be certain, especially when your company is new to whale hunting, that you are not expecting people to just work harder or to work more hours. Be certain that your teams have the resources to handle their existing customers, as well as to add a new whale. If you break the trust with your first whale deal, you may never recover.

- *Velocity:* How fast can you harvest a whale? Most growing companies have internal practices that get in their way. Make improvements by identifying and fixing the top three internal bottlenecks in your harvesting process. Don't try to identify all the problems immediately. Make it manageable. After you repair the top three problems, go on to the next three. Pay particular attention to the flow of work between departments.
- *Scalability:* How many whales can you successfully hunt and harvest each year? Hunting whales requires that your company grow in order for you to harvest new whales. Focus on the fast-growth characteristics that have gotten you where you are today. To ensure growth, stress the development of cross-functional collaboration. Also, learn to be better at allocating your resources. You must be flexible to grow.

These are the decision-making times that will challenge your key management team to excel. If you have all made the commitment to whale hunting, now you must all make the comparable commitment to serving the whale at the highest level of excellence.

Accelerating Capacity and Velocity

Acceleration is the difference between a four-cylinder Civic and a V-8 Jag. Both can cruise at highway speeds, but only one can gain more speed while it's already moving fast. In the business world, the desire to move faster often causes management to exercise more central control. One foot on the gas, one set of hands on the wheel, one eye on the road and one on the rear-view mirror. It's a one-person show—too risky to share.

Yet think of how high-performing racing teams generate speed by collaboration. The precise tuning of the chassis, the engine, the tires; the intense communication between the driver and the crew chief; the orchestrated efforts of the pit crew. These teams prove that acceleration and collaboration go hand in hand.

Accelerating collaborative teamwork is a core promise of whale hunting. And we have argued throughout this book that only a collaborating village can hunt and harvest whales. We understand that you will be challenged to maintain a collaborative culture when a new whale is beached. You must work fast to prove to the whale your capability to deliver on all promises. Yet increased collaboration is equally important. Whenever a boat brings a whale to the beach, the village needs to increase its speed of work immediately. Excuses, rationales, reasons—they pale against the reality of a ready whale on the beach for harvest.

But one of the hardest problems our clients face is accelerating their processes, especially when they are trying to involve many people. Everyone buys the promise of moving faster. Almost everyone wants to accelerate their learning and implementation of promising new processes that will increase their sales, delivery, revenue, and profits. And they tout the benefits of collaboration—buy-in from the team, preparing the next generation of managers, knowledge sharing, and building best practices.

Nevertheless, the burden of the every day routinely sabotages the acceleration plan. We get mired in "how we do things." Meetings, checks and balances, approvals, reports, circulation of every plan to everyone. Collaboration seems too clunky, too hard, too slow. So a few people take over and others step back. When that happens, the village is not ready for whales.

If you want to energize your progress through speed and collaborative decision-making, you need to streamline your collaboration tactics. Here are ten practices to move forward fast:

1. *Define the purpose.* The only reason to collaborate across departmental or divisional lines is to increase the likelihood of good decision making. Collaboration isn't about keeping everyone informed about everything. It's about getting the right information to the right people at the right time so that the organization makes decisive judgments based on collective knowledge.

2. *Keep moving.* Set the schedule of meetings, events, and deliverables up front. The desire for a face-to-face meeting represents the most common procrastination excuse for a collaborative team. Is there ever a time when all members of a 12- or 20-member cross-functional team can promise to be present? Very likely not! Keep to the schedule regardless of who cannot attend. Send someone in your place. Bring one another up to speed. But don't slow the process.

3. *Use an online communication space.* Share ideas, working papers, comments, drafts, and concerns in an online discussion—a

Web-based or server-based solution, a simple e-mail bulletin board, or an internal service. Many useful technologies are available to support information sharing among people who have difficulty being in the same place at the same time.

4. *Be here now.* When you are with your team, recognize what a precious time that is. Be there totally, with your full attention (no e-mail, cell phones, multitasking). Show up on time. Be prepared.

5. *Meet only to do work.* Meetings are not for reporting, presenting, or sharing. They are *only* for reaching decisions based on previously shared materials. Circulate reports ahead of time. Share ideas in a chat room; brainstorm via e-mail. Assign someone to organize the findings. Then come together to act on what you've learned.

6. *Focus on the future.* Shared understanding of the past is both impossible and irrelevant. How many meetings digress to a rehearsal of past attempts, failures, and shortcomings? A fast collaborative team is driven by a powerful shared vision of how good things are going to be when we get this next bit of work completed. Don't shortchange the future by rehashing the past.

7. *Build and test models.* Models are representations of the "real thing." They have the characteristics of the system you are trying to build on a smaller, cheaper, scale. Simulations, games, process charts, 3-D versions, analogies, drawings—all of these models allow you to test ideas, processes, and practices before you implement.

8. *Communicate frugally.* Send information promptly to key teams whose work is affected by your progress. Focus on the commitments (who agreed to do what, in what time frame) and the action items (what needs to happen next). Don't glut the system

with extensive minutes and meeting notes that no one will read. We have heard people complain that no one had time to take minutes, and the next meeting could not be held until minutes were ready. Just the lack of time to produce minutes is a detractor to acceleration.

9. *Embrace progress, not perfection.* Think again of those racing teams. They measure progress in a quarter turn of the wrench, a .10 increase in speed, a one-step quicker tire change. Everything that they deal with is variable; they are in a constant flux to get the most speed out of their driver and their equipment under a given set of conditions, most of which are beyond their control (heat, rain, inspection lines) and change by the day, hour, and minute. Take one step ahead today; take another step ahead next week. You don't need to do it all at once.

10. *There is no "they."* We have sat through countless painful, unproductive meetings in which every proposed action is impeded by the phrase "they'll never approve that." Or, "we can try it, but they'll shoot it down." "They" may be managers, employees, other departments, customers, board members—you name it. "They" are *in charge*. And because "they" are *in charge*, "we" let ourselves off the hook of decisiveness. What could your committee—task force—team—leadership group accomplish if you simply assumed that "they" are "you"?

Your Intake Process

Once you have established an attitude that is welcoming to big new business, you should put together a well-organized, well-documented process for making sure all of your villagers know their roles in this harvest. Start by bringing together all employees, making them aware that the whale is coming. Alert them to how important this new account is to the future of the company and to their personal future. Remind them that the village eats because it hunts! Don't let them find out about this important event through the rumor mill. Motivate them and get them involved from the beginning.

Put together a clear, complete list of the steps needed to harvest the whale. Give everybody and every department a job. Spell it out clearly and in detail. Lay out the timeline. Estimate how long each step will take.

You need a very collaborative process to create intake documents. Let's say you are the harpooner—you've been orchestrating your boat to land this deal; it's your customer and your deal, and you want to make sure that all of the promises you've committed are going to be fulfilled. Or maybe you are the shaman or the village chief. Whatever your personal role, you have been very involved up until this point. Now you face another key internal challenge—how to hand off leadership of this whale-deal to the people in your company who are responsible for fulfilling it.

Nothing is harder—or more important—than the internal handoffs from one phase of whale hunting to the next. If you have had a truly cross-functional boat, some of your subject matter experts will now be the leaders of beaching the whale. They will know some of their counterparts and will have established important relationships. The harpooner, the shaman, and the chief need to back off—monitoring the intake process but allowing your intake team to get to know and to provide service to the new whale team, who have taken over from the buyers' table.

But regardless of how skilled you become in the handoff, it will remain true that many new players, from the whale and from your internal team, will now need to come together to fulfill the contract. The people who buy and sell the deals are not the same people who receive and implement the products and services. Beaching the whale is an opportunity to demonstrate your company's extraordinary attention to the details of a new account, yielding a fast ramp-up for the new business and capturing the rewards sooner rather than later. It's also an opportunity to allow internal inconsistencies, communication lapses, or competition to sabotage a deal that seemed to be done.

We'll just ask a few simple questions here. While the ink is drying on your contract, what happens next? Who from your company makes the first call to someone at the whale? Do you have control over that decision? Are you executing your control? Can you predict with confidence when that call will be made? Are you confident about your escalation procedures? How soon will you learn if anything is going wrong? How much control can you expect on the match between your contractual obligations and the new whale team's expectations? Can you trust that your team will not deliver substantially more—or less—than what you sold?

All of these questions and concerns should be part of your discussions with cross-functional teams that are collaborating to sell and service whale-sized accounts. Do not fear the questions and the possible pitfalls. Fear, rather, the failure to raise and discuss issues of concern.

Prepare an Intake Document

Your internal intake document is a clear explanation of all the steps in the process of on-boarding a new large account. It should be prepared routinely by an individual or team who bears responsibility for completing and circulating the document within a fixed time frame. The generic version will be customized for each new whale.

Include vital information about the implementation teams on both sides of the deal. Gather and include the basic information, like addresses, phone numbers, duties, and so forth, of the whale's implementation team. The document should also name your implementation people and which members of this group are responsible for each major step in the harvest.

The preparation alone of the intake document adds value. The simple preparation process will flush out problems you are about to face before you go live. Rules for preparation also prevent you from trying to wing it during any part of the launch. Preparing formal intake documents can help you anticipate confusion about who is responsible for any step in the process and can reveal if anyone disagrees with the timing of any planned move.

Our client, Power Direct, has a detailed intake document that guides their process of bringing a new call center client on board. It's a workable management tool because it identifies the responsible departments, delineates their responsibility, and requires a sign-off date and manager's approval. See Table 9.1.

The department of client services has ownership of on-boarding a new customer at Power Direct. In addition to the table of activities listed in the table, there is another list of expectations for bringing a new client on board, as detailed here:

- Communicate with the client and obtain information to ensure campaign success.
- Schedule a setup meeting (include each department manager).
- Create a process flow with the client and communicate with each department.
- Send an e-mail to each department manager including all responsibilities and time frames.

Table 9.1 Client Services Checklist

Campaign Name:

Contact Name/Number:

Department	Responsibility	Date Signed	Department Manager Completed Initials
Sales and Client Services	Signed agreement (give to Finance) Set up meeting (e-mail all) Important dates (e-mail all) Collect the setup fees (give to Finance) Capture historical information—scripts, reports, etc. (e-mail all) Discuss data/leads needed Gather contact information Set clear expectations		
Client and Client Services	Sales process flow (e-mail all) Approve a script—14 days needed (give to IT) Billing needs (give to Finance) Data/leads (give to IT; discuss the quantity with Operations) Reporting needs Marketing examples and dates Campaign hours of operation Output file needs (coordinate with IT) Create the disposition needs (Give to IT and Operations)		

(Continued)

Table 9.1 (*Continued*)

			Department Manager Completed Initials

Campaign Name:

Contact Name/Number:

Department	Responsibility	Date Signed	Department Manager Completed Initials
Operations and Client Services	Create a bonus structure (give to Finance) Staffing needs (give to HR) Hours of operations (give to HR)		
HR and Client Services	Recruiting needs Background checks Job responsibilities/requirements		
IT and Software Client Services	Scripting Create a Dynacall task Voicemail setup Create sales output file Test output files System access——e-mail, fax maker, etc. Create dispositions programming Unique telephone number requirements Create desktop documents Order management system (if needed) Script testing (Education must test 24 hours prior to launch)		

Education and Client Services	Create education packet (give to Operations) Scheduled training dates (give to HR) Schedule classroom times Test scripts 24 hours prior to launch		
QA and Client Services	Monitoring needs (give to Operations) Schedule a conference call with the client, QA and Operations		
Finance and Client Survives	Invoicing/pricing Compensation structure Copy agreement Collect setup fees		
IT	Hardware requirements Computers Telephones Partitions Wiring		

- Create business rules and discuss with each department.
- Verify each step is completed.
- E-mail weekly updates to all department managers (include all responsibilities that have been completed and still need follow-up).
- Ensure all preceding steps are completed within the allotted time frames.

This example illustrates the level of detail that one company requires to carry forward the promises of the sales cycle to the realities of the product and service delivery.

Meritocracy

Beaching the whale requires that all members of your employee team be on board enthusiastically. This phase is bound to highlight the need for significant cultural changes in your company. It is also the time when you should expect to encounter resistance, so we offer this discussion of how to reposition your company as a meritocracy, if it is not already thus.

The Arctic North is a brutal environment, leaving little room for error for anyone living there. The incredibly cold and harsh climate will not tolerate mistakes. Whale hunting villages can ill afford to have members fail to bring back a whale, ignore or miss the signs of predators like wolves or polar bears, or be unready to act when all hands are needed. Life and death is an extremely efficient arbiter of merit.

For your company to sustain fast growth, a meritocracy is crucial. Firms that stall in their development can be weighed down by other forms of cultural management. But how do you shift from a "benevolent monarchy" or a "parliamentary" style of leadership to one governed by individual performance? The first step is a clear definition. A meritocracy must meet certain requirements to warrant the designation. A meritocracy should be governed by the following:

- Clearly defined drivers of success for the organization and individuals
- Accountability attached to responsibility, and vice versa
- Clearly understood consequences for both incidental and consistent failure
- Clearly understood rewards for meritorious performance

Firms that have grown quickly have often done so as a result of extremely hard work and loyalty. In the movie *Castaway*, a generational family of FedEx employees sits around the holiday meal recounting when Fred Smith and the team sorted the first deliveries by hand on card tables in a garage. This kind of kinship illustrates the way many firms feel about "the good old days."

Due to the needs of the business, fast-growth companies rarely start with what they believe are nonessentials such as personnel manuals, formal mentoring programs, and clear individual performance and development plans. The theory is simple: "If we make it to the point that we are a real company, we will have the time to figure all that stuff out."

Unfortunately, the time for imposing the regimen and discipline of a more mature organization comes and goes, and the company remains committed to its "fast and loose" approach. Without the best people in the best positions to leverage their abilities, sustaining growth is very difficult.

A guiding principle for a meritocracy should be assigning value exclusively to performance. A process might look like this:

1. *Review or draft objective job descriptions for all positions.* Although this may seem obvious, the lack of written descriptions, including performance objectives, plagues many fast-growth companies.
2. *Determine the major leverage points in organizational performance.* Companies often look to only financial performance indicators. However, customer satisfaction, employee satisfaction, time to delivery, errors per thousand, waste, and other key indicators are also important. Pick those factors that drive short- and long-term performance, and decide how each position contributes to those factors.
3. *Work with current staff to establish baseline expectations.* Benchmarking has been a key to all performance improvement. Establishing the metrics for current levels of performance will be difficult, but necessary, if this measurement does not already exist.
4. *Organize the company around an objective evaluation of personnel and company needs.* You need to avoid the mistake of reorganizing first and then determining best fits. Take the time to follow the process systematically, to avoid making mistakes in placement and definition.
5. *Communicate, communicate, communicate.* Change is difficult for everyone. The rationale for change and the expected improvement needs to be clearly articulated.
6. *Recognize the value of each individual's investment.* Too often, change in organizational structure comes as a punishment for perceived failure. Restructuring a company to a meritocracy must avoid assigning blame by focusing on opportunity and fit.

Long-term employees and founding friends are important to the past and future of a firm. Separating the value of the past from the potential of the future will pay dividends for all involved. Fast-growth companies that follow a systematic approach to developing a meritocracy will shorten dramatically the time for such change to take place.

Talk to the Whale

All of our advice in this chapter relates to your internal processes and procedures. And it is critically important to get your team totally on board and to manage the intake process in every detail.

But one more point is equally important. And that is, let the whale know what you are doing! We have observed so many clients working fitfully and faithfully upon signing a new deal with a whale. All of the internal intake processes are being developed, reviewed, ratified, and trained. Sometimes, as we would always propose, the entire village is attuned to the knowledge that a whale is coming. There is a great deal of enthusiasm and an extensive amount of important cross-functional planning. In fact, everything that we would hope to see in beaching a whale is going on at a high level.

However, while all of this activity is going on inside your business, is anyone talking to the whale? Are you letting them know what you are doing, how it fits into your service to them, what they could contribute to this planning process? While you are beaching your whale, internal communication with your village and external communications with the whale will increase the odds of your success. The same tides and winds that brought your whale to the beach could take it right out to sea if you do not work quickly and maintain vigilance.

In the next chapter, we discuss the importance of making certain that your business has a culture that will allow it to complete the harvest successfully.

Beach the Whale Action Items

- *Prepare your village to harvest the whale efficiently and appropriately.*
- *Take all necessary steps to accelerate your capacity and the velocity of your work.*
- *Complete your whale hunting maps for all of the intake processes, to ensure that the whale experiences a seamless and reassuring transition.*
- *Align the reward system for your villagers with your expectations of how they will handle new work.*
- *Communicate with your whale, to allay its fears.*

Please visit www.thewhalehunters.com to download the sales process tools introduced in this chapter.

10

Honor the Whale

ONCE THE WHALE WAS BEACHED, the entire village went to work to harvest it. Everyone had a well-defined role, which was pursued quickly and skillfully. There was no time to waste. The youngest children, from the age of four, were taught to harvest whale oil from the blubber. Whale oil was the first commercially viable animal or mineral oil. The Inuit used it as fuel for lamps. It also represented wealth; beyond the village's own needs, excess oil could be stored and traded for other goods.

The whale meat was divided and packaged, to be preserved and stored. All other parts of the whale would also be used in some fashion—especially the bone. Over the years, the Inuit had developed very sophisticated tools and procedures to harvest all of the components. Sometimes the rib cage of bone was used to support a tunnel from the ice to the interior hut for the next winter. Whale bone and teeth or baleen were often carved or etched in intricate patterns known as scrimshaw.

The spoils of the hunt were divided among the villagers. Those families that contributed the most—provided the umiak, for example, or harpooned the whale—were rewarded with a larger share of the whale's bounty. It was a society in which families could build wealth through hard work and clever innovation. Nevertheless, all who participated in scouting, hunting, or harvesting also shared in the food and other materials that the whale provided.

The Modern Whale Harvest

Landing a whale deal may seem simple in the face of actually delivering on your promises to the whale. Whether you provide services or products, whether you are a manufacturer or a distributor, whether you fulfill this contract by shipping pieces of something to the whale or by working face to face with the whale to implement a new system or service, you are at risk of failure.

We imagine that most readers of this book are on the sales and business development side of the equation—you are the harpooner, or the shaman, or the chief. If so, we suspect that you have experienced your share of frustration at your company's inability to service properly an account that you have landed.

One of our basic premises is that to be a fast-growth company, your company will need to be able to land and harvest whales as a steady diet. That is, the exceptionally large account that comes in tomorrow will be a test case for your readiness to handle another one, and another one, until it all becomes routine.

We also believe that landing and harvesting whales will transform your company. You will have the opportunity to grow in capacity and to excel in delivery on promises. If you continue to meet and exceed your promises at increasingly high levels of sales, you are on the road to rapid, sustainable growth.

The core characteristics of your company's ability to deliver on promises to whales have everything to do with your company culture. For you to fulfill the promises you made during your sales process, you will need to be supported by a culture of fast growth among your delivery teams. Let's explore what that means and how you can influence it.

At this stage of the deal, you need to know that your internal operations and customer service teams are ready to accept a warm handoff, and bring to the whale the same level of attention that you've provided during the first seven phases of the Whale Hunters' Process. We discussed in the last chapter how to align your reward system with your growth expectations. And we discussed planning and communication and intake documents. Yet you may have many of these things in place and still experience among your staff an unwillingness, or a lack of readiness, or a slowness to complete the harvest of a big new account. If that has been your experience, we encourage you to pay increasing attention to the attributes of your company culture.

A Fast-Growth Culture

For a fast-growing company finding it difficult to move into the next echelon of sales and growth, whale hunting can be an answer. We have found that the differences between healthy, fast-growth companies, which are successful at hunting whales, and troubled firms, which generally fail in their efforts, depend on the two key variables of a fast-growth culture: *collaboration* and *resources*.

Collaboration is the ease and efficiency with which people within your company share knowledge and work together for a common purpose. Resources are the money, time, personnel, and technology available to accomplish the company's goals. Both of these variables depend more on your teams' perception of their presence than they depend on any validated evidence. That is, do your people believe that they are working in a collaborative environment? And even more important, do they perceive that your company lives in a culture of abundant resources rather than a culture of scarcity? If you promise to your employees that whenever you bring on a new whale, you will correspondingly increase such requirements as staffing, warehousing, data management, reporting, and so forth, do you deliver on that promise? Or do you expect an already hard-working team to incorporate huge new business without corresponding investments? In your early whale hunts, it's a good idea to err on the side of generosity in providing resources to your team.

To determine if yours is a healthy, growth-oriented company, consider the culture grid shown here.

Culture Grid

High	Sustaining Culture/ Bureaucratic	Fast-Growth Culture
Resources		
	Declining Culture/ Internally Competitive	Emerging Culture/ Entrepreneurial
Low		High

Collaboration

In the lower right-hand section of the grid we illustrate an "emerging" culture. Most new companies begin life in this entrepreneurial category, often with meager resources but marked by enthusiastic collaboration among the excited and motivated employees. Their start-up culture is high energy with a noticeable can-do attitude. Workers at all levels consider themselves invested in the success of the company and behave like stakeholders. Clients drive company decisions. A team-based decision-making process empowers all of the employees. Job responsibilities may be fluid. While money is tight and hours are long, the entire team celebrates each success and works together to build the company.

But these can be precarious times. The emerging company runs the risk of letting inefficiencies creep in, wasting key resources. Before you can acquire significant resources, you may begin to lose the valuable collaboration culture among employees that has helped you to grow and to thrive. Entrepreneurial companies need to build on their successes by establishing replicable processes that can be used again and again to land and service significant customer accounts. These processes at many points of growth require more professional management, more role definition and specification, more distribution of knowledge and authority.

Unless you are actively managing your company's culture, the natural progress of an entrepreneurial company is toward the bottom left of the culture grid—into a declining culture that we define as internally competitive.

Signs of an internally competitive environment include a rigid, formal management structure. Increasing divisions within the workforce begin creating a perceived need for more and more line managers to compete for resources and recognition. Although some CEOs have been taught to view internal competition among their VPs as a way to identify the highest performers, collaboration always suffers as internal competition increases.

Here's how you need to think about it. Today's business environment changes at lightning speed. It is a global culture in which rewards accrue to business leaders and their companies that are agile, quick to decide and to move. Agile decision-making requires lots of cross-functional collaboration. How can finance make a big decision about adding personnel unless human resources is on board regarding the opportunities to hire and the costs of hiring? How can operations plan for growth without understanding the personnel needs and the costs of meeting those needs?

Internally competitive companies are vulnerable to external threats and run the risk of spending all their time putting out fires instead of anticipating future needs. The energy required to regain the entrepreneurial spirit in a company that has fallen into a declining culture is exhausting.

If the internally competitive firm does not fail, it may develop into the sustaining culture of a bureaucracy. The bureaucratic company has continued to grow and, in the process, has acquired resources. If you are fortunate enough to have a world-class R&D operation, a savvy marketing team, and operational excellence, coupled with a set of products or services that match your market at a given place and time, your internally competitive company may achieve a position in the upper-left quadrant of our culture grid.

Bureaucracies are stable and therefore confident. However, they are slow-moving. They often miss important opportunities because of their slow response time and resistance to change. Processes become stagnant, and there is too little collaboration to permit agility and market readiness. Business literature is replete with examples of bureaucracies that failed, as well as those that successfully reinvented themselves. The reinvention process involves finding a way to instigate the characteristics of fast growth.

Where Are You on the Culture Grid?

Culture of Scarcity

- *Attends to deficits.*
- *People focus on their needs.*
- *People hoard knowledge and expertise.*

Culture of Abundance

- *Attends to assets.*
- *People focus on their contributions.*
- *People invest their knowledge and expertise.*

Culture of Bureaucracy

- *Attends to entitlement.*
- *Decisions and work habits are slow.*
- *People focus on time for money.*

Culture of Entrepreneurship

- *Attends to earnings.*
- *Decisions and work habits are energetic.*
- *People focus on their results.*

Culture of Competition

- *Attends to winners and losers.*
- *People work in silos.*
- *Rewards warriors and rock stars.*

Culture of Collaboration

- *Attends to how the team wins.*
- *People collaborate well.*
- *Rewards high-performing teams and leaders.*

Building a Fast-Growth Culture

For the purpose of whale hunting, the best cultural alternative is the fast-growth category. We'd like to see an entrepreneurial company bypass internal competition and bureaucracy by moving deliberately and directly into the fast-growth quadrant. The right balance is found between a high level of resources and a high level of collaboration. The fast-growth company integrates the best of an entrepreneurial spirit with the desire to implement reliable processes that are continually reviewed and improved. In a fast-growth company, decision making occurs at all levels, yet there is still a clear escalation process. Change is a core competency. Leaders and employees understand how to balance quick reaction time with a sense of overall control that reduces panic and builds confidence. In a fast-growth company culture, sales and operations are well aligned, and the entire company is focused on consistent growth. If your company is not currently in this quadrant of the culture cube, the lessons of this book will help you to make the necessary transitions.

Culture Exercises

If you are going to be prepared to harvest a steady diet of whales, you will need a high-performing cross-functional leadership team. You will need this collaboration at the levels of senior management; but even more important, you will need to translate this expectation to the next management level and to all of your employees. If you are going to launch a series of boats with the right subject matter experts accompanying the harpooner and shaman, you will need buy-in from management in all of those areas where subject matter experts work—and they work in every area of your company. You have to have the flexibility to put a team together to visit a whale or to host a whale's visit to your site. You need people who can cover for each other so that one can be involved in a sales process.

We include two activities that your internal village teams can use to assess their contributions to a fast-growth culture. In our experience, people fail to collaborate not because they do not want to but because they do not understand why they should or how they should. Try these activities with your team.

Identify Assets

In the first example, a leadership team identifies what it perceives to be deficits in its performance with respect to whale hunting. Once you've identified deficits, you can define the desirable asset that you'd like to achieve. Next, list all of the obstacles that are in your way of transforming deficits to assets. Finally, create strategies for overcoming the obstacles. This activity should yield a robust set of strategies to transform at least a few deficits into assets. Table 10.1 gives an example.

The next activity encourages department-based teams to explore the assets they can contribute to whale hunting, and to make these concrete by citing specific examples.

Classify Assets

Table 10.2 is a list of whale hunting assets that may exist in your department. For each category, identify at least three examples of an asset.

When each department has identified and given examples of its assets, bring team representatives together across departmental

Table 10.1 Eliminate Deficits

1. Identify Whale Hunting Deficits in Your Area	2. What is the Opposite Asset?	3. List Obstacles to Transforming Deficits to Assets	4. Create Strategies for Overcoming the Obstacles
Lack of knowledge about upcoming sales	Up-to-date knowledge about sales and market pipelines	Lack of process Poor communication Lack of energy Forecast is not good Firefighting	Create a tracking system. Reorganize and upgrade the forecast documents. Develop common assumptions. Management team takes ownership and responsibility for communication.
Lack of strategic market research	An active process for strategic market analysis	Lack of determination	Fund a position and create an active process.
Insufficient time to train new staff	Good advance information on capacity needs Rapid, effective training methods	Weak forecasting— see above	Reliable capacity predictions

boundaries to review the asset classification and to determine how best to use core assets in service to your whales.

Engage the Village

As we've discussed, the Inuit villagers participated in the whale hunt before the boats were launched and after the whale was beached. Their assistance in all of the preparation earned them

Table 10.2 Asset Classification			
Asset	**Example**	**Example**	**Example**
Reputation			
Skill			
Knowledge			
History			
People			
Financial resources			
Relationships			
Connectivity			
Other			

a vested interest in the result of the hunt. During the hunt, their prayers, songs, and chants were seen as vital. And their proper and timely work in the harvest was seen as essential.

It is the same in the complex sales transaction. The entire company needs to be involved in and informed of all facets of the sale. They shouldn't just be brought in after the fact. If the village is to feel part of the process, they must *be* part of the process.

The subject matter experts who are assigned to a boat should be the leaders in engaging the rest of the village. They should use other people in their departments as much as possible to help them prepare for their roles in the boat. And they should keep others informed of the progress of the deal. Let them celebrate the forward movement and mounting excitement so that when the account is finalized they greet it with enthusiasm and a satisfaction that come only through participation.

It is very powerful when a subject matter expert comes back from a visit to the whale and is able to say, "I met Anthony, who is one of the project managers for IT installation, and it will be easy to work with him once we have closed this deal." This process differs from the typical manner in which sales is responsible for selling, and no one else knows what's in the pipeline until it arrives.

But beyond participation, in this phase, strict timing is important. In the Inuit hunt, everyone understood that the meat had to be removed from the carcass, divided into movable pieces, and preserved in the frozen earth before it began to deteriorate. Likewise, your village needs to be prepared to move quickly.

If you prepare thoroughly, meet your promises, make the appropriate investments to service this big new deal, your company will get stronger, faster, and more accustomed to whales. You will transform to a higher level of capability in ways that you may not have imagined yet. For example, when your smaller company does business with a much larger company, your people learn a lot about process and management of big assignments from their counterpart teams who are managing the account on the whale's side.

Risk Management

You face a 90-day period when miscommunication and vulnerability in your village can destroy a new deal. Of course, 90 days is an arbitrary time frame. The exact time period for your deal varies based on the type of product or service you sell and the type and size of your new whale customer. Nevertheless, you need to pay heightened attention for at least 30 days prior to the date you begin implementation and 60 days after that date.

The 30 days prior to the formal implementation date is a time to head off problems. In this period of time after the sale and before the delivery, it is very easy to focus inwardly, with everyone spending time and attention on preparing for the delivery. But if you reduce your contact with the whale, the whale may get nervous. This is a serious mistake. If you're the harpooner or shaman, maintain your contacts with the whale and help in the transition to your delivery team and the whale's team. While things might be going according to plan on your side, if the customer isn't aware of the moves you are making, the assumption might be made that nothing is happening. Be certain that you have a detailed plan for communication with the whale prior to the contract's start date. This plan may include which of your villagers will contact which people at the whale and for what purpose.

This 30-day period is also the time to confirm and reconfirm any specifications that the whale considers important. Do careful quality tests of all your products and procedures and test runs of all your plans. Don't wait to find out about weaknesses under live conditions. Perhaps you can create the product prototype or service model under as close to actual conditions as possible and have the whale examine and approve it. If you have promised training as part of your delivery, start it as early as possible. If you need to gather information from people who work at the whale, start gathering it.

Make and Keep Promises

One of the best ways to cement a relationship with a new whale is to make specific promises and keep them. Remember that whales are afraid of you. Reduce their fear by demonstrating consistency and process control. We like to say make and keep three promises.

For example:

- "I will have these specs to you on March 13." And on March 13 you deliver the specs and call to confirm that they were received and understood.
- Or, "Janet from our human resources department will provide you with the names, phone numbers, and e-mail addresses for the six new employees we are hiring to work on your account. We will have these employees on board three weeks from today." And three weeks from today Janet sends the information and calls to confirm that it was received and is acceptable.
- Or, "I will arrange a conference call for your implementation team with our account managers for IT and help desk services. We will get this scheduled tomorrow and we will hold the call before the end of next week." And tomorrow you schedule the call and by the end of next week, you have completed it, documented it, shared information with everyone who was involved, and reported back to the whale that this call has been completed.

These are simple signs of having things under control. We understand that probably you don't have things as well under control as you would like when you land a whale. So while you are working feverishly on the inside to deliver what you sold, do a good job of managing the communication by making and keeping promises.

The counterpart, of course, is to avoid making a promise that you can't keep or that you fail to keep. That's very damaging, and it's why everyone in your village needs to understand their roles and responsibilities in completing this harvest.

Handoffs

Whale hunting in the harvest phase is completely compatible with operational and manufacturing process improvement initiatives such as kaizen, Six Sigma, and lean manufacturing. We are focused on the sales process, which we believe by definition must include the processes for delivering what has been sold; but if your company requires serious improvements to its abilities to deliver, you will need to deal with them in concert with your whale hunting activities. While the boat is out on the ocean hunting a whale, the villagers continue to prepare for the harvest.

A simple but extremely important process improvement is to explore with a cross-functional team the boundaries or "space" between one department and another as your company services the whale.

- Do you have a formal process by which the harpooner hands off this new whale to a key account manager or to an operational director or to a customer service representative?
- Are these procedures written down?
- Have you identified the owner for each step?
- Have you defined the time frame in which the step must be completed?
- Does the process include what information must be shared and with whom and by when and in what format?

As you complete the harvest, you want to release the harpooner and shaman as soon as possible to hunt another whale. If your company is weak on delivery, the harpooner and shaman often become the de facto account managers for the whale. People on the whale's team will call the harpooner when they have questions or concerns because that's the person they know and have learned to trust.

Good handoffs greatly increase your efficiency and your professionalism in the eyes of the whale. But good handoffs by their nature require a high level of collaboration among managers in different departments. You began to build this collaborative approach to whale hunting when you populated your boat with subject matter experts from a variety of areas. These people have already established relationships with their whale counterparts, so continue to keep them visible and in responsible roles during the handoffs.

A Preimplementation Summit

Provide an opportunity for your company to cement your image with the new whale customer by planning and executing a preimplementation summit between your company and the whale. It can be a time for introductions, facility tours, information exchange, or a host of items that vary according to your business and what you have sold. It provides a time to anticipate problems that need to be dealt with early. And it gives you cues about how accessible the whale's personnel will be. If people do not attend, contact them. Get them back into the fold. Answer their concerns. Ease their fears.

Postimplementation Planning

During the 60 days following implementation, you will continue the high level of communication and reporting. The shaman and harpooner will remain engaged to ensure that handoffs are complete and smooth. By the nature of a whale-sized deal, it will take time to fulfill your delivery, even if you sell widgets. We presume that if you sell a deal for 10 to 20 times the number of widgets that you typically produce, you will, at the least, need some time to manufacture all those additional widgets, and ship them, and service them. It's likely that your deal is to deliver widgets to many different locations in certain quantities for a period of years. If you sell a service, your delivery may also occur over months or years for a big deal.

If you fail in any way during the first 60 days, you jeopardize the deal for the long term. The whale may not fire you but will find ways to slow down the ramp-up of your services, or cut back on the products and services they want, or introduce other contractors that you will be expected to work with. You do not want any of these outcomes. Work hard to take countermeasures for success.

Fighting Barnacles

What if you have employees who interfere with the company's new, streamlined, fast, and efficient approach? We call them *barnacles*.

From the ancient Inuit umiak to the newly christened *George H. W. Bush* aircraft carrier, barnacles have been nothing but trouble for boats. You know barnacles—those passive predators that attach to the bottom of your boat and interfere with its performance.

In its larva form, a barnacle has to locate a permanent environment that appears to be safe—else it will die. When it picks a suitable spot, often the bottom of a boat, the larva fastens itself headfirst to the surface. If not forcibly removed, it is cemented to that surface for the rest of its life. And it grows. It brings its friends and neighbors along, and they grow too.

That mass causes boats to lose speed and maneuverability, so wise sailors for centuries have been careful to keep their boats moving, lift them out of the water when not in use, and scrape barnacles from the hull when prevention fails.

When you hunt and harvest a whale, you can't afford to carry barnacles with you. We define barnacles as dissonant employee behaviors that grow, attract others, and disrupt the course and speed of your boat. For a successful hunt, you will need to keep them from attaching to the boat or scrape them from the bottom of the boat as soon as you recognize them. How can you recognize the barnacles? Four versions are described here.

The Camouflage Barnacle

These barnacles are bright and attentive during meetings, and vocally supportive of whatever you suggest. If asked about the project's feasibility, they will respond, "Yes, that is certainly possible." Sometimes they have positions of authority within the hunt. They always seem to be working, often cheerfully, on whatever project you've given them. They attend meetings, develop charts, and present reports.

Yet their part of the harvest never seems to move forward. Or parts of it will move forward, but the whole is never connected. They manage to make known throughout the company that others are preventing them from completing their work. They are extremely hard to spot and can only be identified by their behavior, not by outward appearances. Yet they are still barnacles and therefore immensely destructive. They present themselves as part of the boat and can remain there for many years, slowly but surely keeping the whale hunting process from being sharp, clear, and successful.

The Cheapskate Barnacle

The cheapskate barnacles are the employees who believe the cheapest is always the best. These employees will gripe about the amount of money being spent to hunt whales. They will point out to their coworkers things that could have been purchased with the money being expended. Cheapskate barnacles will predict failure and will remark about the time being wasted on a losing cause. You may hear them say, "Just send that money to my department, and see what we can do with it!"

Only a small amount of time is needed for this kind of complaint to attach itself firmly to the boat and attract others. Rumors will begin to float that raises will be smaller this year because of this whale hunt. Resources will be constrained. Soon there will be many conversations in the hallways that begin like this: "Yeah, I think this is a wonderful project, but . . ." or "It would be wonderful if this could really happen, but . . ."

The Way We Were Barnacle

The third type of barnacle adopts the role of unofficial historian and keeper of the culture. The way we were barnacles will say, "That's not the way we've always done it," or "That's not how we do it here." As your company takes up whale hunting as a deliberate strategy, you will make changes in how you conduct business. A whale is not the usual kind of sale. And the ways that have worked in the past are not going to work in this instance. Change is difficult although necessary. These employees, however, regard change as a negative reflection on what has been going on in the company. They do not understand that the accomplishments of the past have created your current whale-hunting capacities. The way we were barnacles prefer hunting seals, mistrust anything out of the ordinary, and express nostalgia for earlier days, when:

- "The CEO knew everyone in the company by name."
- "We had a personal relationship with our customers, not such a businesslike one."
- "We didn't take such risks."
- "We didn't all have to be involved in sales."
- "We were like a family and weren't so wrapped up in making money. We loved just making our widgets."

The Doomsday Barnacle

The final type of barnacle is the custodian of past failures. As whale hunting is introduced, doomsday barnacles respond in this way: "We tried that once before, and it didn't work." Never mind that times, employees, attitudes, possibilities, knowledge, markets, and even the company itself have all changed since then. These employees are so fond of their position that they will tell anyone who will stand still and listen about the many efforts that have been made in the past to do this very thing. And how they have all failed. The more spectacular the failure, the more the doomsday barnacle delights in retelling it.

Barnacle Control

If you are going to hunt whales, be scrupulous about maintaining your boat and your harvest. Watch for barnacles and do not allow them to attach themselves to your boat. If you discover barnacles on the hull, be diligent in removing them. It is not productive to try to change employee attitudes, but when those attitudes lead to behavior—and that includes vocal behavior—that threatens the boat's maneuverability, they must be scraped from the boat.

Prevent barnacles by refusing to provide a safe haven for them. Your associates and employees can point to "barnacle behavior" with unfailing accuracy. They are watching to see if you recognize the same characteristics that they observe. And most important, they are watching to see if you will preserve your boat or threaten its safety by permitting barnacles to make it slow and clumsy.

The smooth, efficient, and effective division of responsibilities that the harvest requires takes many different forms in many different companies. Nevertheless, it is characterized by a culture of planning, collaboration, and the desire to improve service to the whale. After the harvest, the village celebrates.

Honor the Whale Action Items

- *Engage your village to build a fast-growth culture.*
- *Make and keep promises to demonstrate your reliability to the whale.*
- *Improve handoffs at all junctures in your village.*
- *Hold a predelivery summit with the whale to ensure smooth implementation.*
- *Control barnacles—don't let any villager undermine the village's performance.*

Please visit www.thewhalehunters.com to download the sales process tools introduced in this chapter.

11

Celebrate the Whale

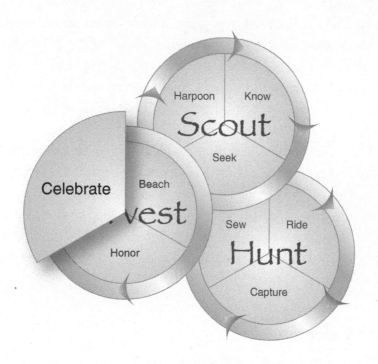

ONCE THE VILLAGERS had completed their harvest of all of the meat, bone, blubber, and other usable parts of the whale, had stored all the fruits of their labor, cleaned their tools, and packed everything to return to their village, they were undoubtedly ready to celebrate.

But it might surprise you to know that they did not celebrate the brave harpooners, or the wise shaman, or the clever hunters who made up the crew. They did not celebrate the village or the villagers. Instead, they celebrated the whale. To them, the whale was a gift from the gods, the source of sustenance for the people of their village.

By tradition, the Inuit kept the whale's head intact during the harvest. When the work was done, a crew in an umiak would tow the whale's head back into the deeper waters of the sea and release it. There, they would watch it sink deep into the black waters with the belief that it would be reborn, to return another spring. This action completed an eternal cycle that had sustained the village for another year.

The Inuit didn't view their whale as prey, or an enemy, even though it could have taken their lives. They didn't even see it as the victim of the hunt. They loved and revered the whale. The whale was a participant in this effort to feed and sustain their people. It was a creature to be respected, not distained or feared. The whale was a key participant in their ongoing efforts to survive and to thrive.

Why Celebrate?

Does your village ever celebrate the whale? Do you have engaging, imaginative ways to show the people on the whale side how much you value their business and their trust? By celebrating, we don't mean lavish gifts, fancy dinners for a few key people, or a fruit basket delivered for the holidays. Those are either acceptable or unacceptable within the culture of a particular whale, but they won't set you apart.

Rather, we are talking about a pervasive attitude in your company that the whale is your source of sustenance. The village eats because it hunts. Without the whale, there is no village. How well does your team understand the value of a whale?

We don't pose this as a rhetorical question, because we understand that landing a whale will disrupt your village, create new work, require better processes, and in general make new demands on your company. So it is very easy for the village to get cranky when they are harvesting that whale. And if it is a demanding whale, and hard to deal with, your villagers are even more likely to become disgruntled.

That's in part why it's so important to celebrate the whale. Truly, your company cannot survive without its customers. And equally truly, the more respect your village builds for its customers, the more motivated each individual will be to provide expert and excellent service to the customer.

You also celebrate the whale so that the whale will know it is being celebrated! In the whale-hunting model, this final phase of the process is hugely important. Actually, although we are gathering celebration stories into this chapter, you will see that celebration ideas can be useful throughout the hunt, especially when the whale is visiting your place of business or you are taking a full boat to them.

As you complete this final step of the final phase, remember that you have participated in something big, something important.

Make the completion of this process memorable for everyone inside the new client company and within your own organization. Respect your whale. Help the new customers to realize that they are an important part of your future and you an important part of theirs. Show the whale respect and consideration and you will assure yourself a future of harvest and growth.

Celebrate with the Whale

Your whale must know that you are celebrating it. It's not about spending a lot of money on any kind of quid pro quo; it's about using your team's creativity and imagination to leave an indelible impression on your new customer.

Our client, Langham Logistics, Inc., celebrates its whales as well as anyone we know. We'll give you a few examples here. On one occasion, when Langham was hosting the "big show," they built a wall of all of the whale's products—literally bought these products and stacked them up against a wall, prominently displayed in their headquarters. But that wasn't the celebration. After the products were purchased and displayed, Langham employees were invited to post sticky notes on the products that they use. The note might say, for example, "Hi, I'm Lynn in the warehouse, and my family uses your product every week." The big message was this: We are your customers, and we are looking forward to your becoming a customer of ours! We care, we pay attention, your business matters. A company that will go to some trouble to make this point gets the attention of the whale.

On another occasion, Langham had closed a big deal with a whale, earning the right to be a preferred vendor for transportation services. There was, however, no commitment to placing business, no agreement regarding volumes—nothing but placement on an elite list. Further, the buyers who would purchase services on a daily basis from the preferred vendors were not present at the buyers' table during the sales process. They knew very little about Langham Logistics, Inc. The whale was located in another state, and there was limited opportunity for the buyers to make any connection with Langham's people or services.

Langham and the whale had planned a celebration lunch at the whale's headquarters. Members of Langham's boat would travel to the whale and host the lunch. But they wanted to make an impression on those people who every day make the decisions about which vendor to call for the next shipment. How could Langham get onto a list that was already long, populated by service providers that were good, and whose businesses were stable?

They chose to produce a video postcard, replicating the big show tour that they manage at their headquarters, and share it as a DVD with all of the whale's employees. In this video, Langham's harpooner welcomes the whale to Langham's headquarters building. A series of people introduce themselves, hold up products of the whale that they personally use, and explain their role in proposed service to the whale. It was produced inexpensively in-house, and was informal and appealing in its honesty and straightforward narrative. The best thing about the DVD was that Langham chose to include a set of outtakes—bloopers and blunders—at the end. These scenes reinforced the idea that the setting was real, the people were real, the service promises were real—and that the Langham people had a sense of humor and were not afraid to display it. The DVD was widely circulated among people at the whale's headquarters.

Needless to say, Langham began to get shipping orders from this whale at a rate they had not anticipated. They found a way to take a personal message of appreciation to a large number of people at the whale. They reduced the whale's fear, increased the whale's interest, and celebrated their new relationship with the whale.

Several of our clients have engaged their villages in celebrating the whales during the progress of a hunt. Designed to build commitment to whale hunting and anticipation of new deals with whales, these activities include large-scale whale-hunting process charts, posted in high-visibility areas of their companies, with a tracking system to identify which boats have been launched and which whales the boats are pursuing. Progress is tracked through the nine phases of the whale hunt by moving the boat icon from one phase to another as the deal reaches closure. This practice encourages all members of the village to participate in a hunt, to share their knowledge of the whale, and to celebrate when the whale is landed.

The Whale Hunters have sourced the world for meaningful mementos with which to celebrate our whales. Among our favorites are a brass compass, which we equate to "chart the waters" and a telescope, which we equate to "focus on the hunt." We may give these gifts at an implementation summit, a kickoff, at a holiday, or for no apparent reason. For one of our clients, with upwards of 600 employees, we created a congratulatory poster, packaged it in an appealing way, and distributed it to every employee at multiple locations to coincide with a quarterly reporting meeting.

Our client, WorkPlace Media, experts in the behaviors of the at-work consumer, has instituted a number of in-house awards and recognitions to call the village's attention to a new whale client and thereby to prepare the village to celebrate the client.

One of our clients sent one of their whales a "Blue Chip Award" for excellence, in the form of a huge box of chocolate chip cookies with blue frosting, signifying "we appreciate your business and we celebrate your success."

Our point is that the village celebrates the whale, not its own effort. The hunt succeeded because all the villagers knew and performed their roles. As villagers matured and developed new skills, they took on greater responsibility in the process. They learned how to communicate through patterns, repetition, and example set by leaders within the tribe.

The hunt is a predictable process that minimizes the unknowns. In today's environment, this translates to more energy and focus on the ultimate center of attention—your whale.

Feed Your Ravens

The raven is one of the most important creatures in the life of a whale-hunting village. An animal spirit who serves as a special guide to the shaman and harpooners, the raven personifies the wisdom of past generations to support the best interests of the village.

Today's fast-growth companies focus on the care and feeding of their ravens. The relationship between your company and your raven guides is priceless. Launching a boat is expensive and dangerous, so the shaman seeks guidance from the village's ravens, who can help to determine the whale's readiness and how to approach the whale. Once the deal is done, the ravens can continue to counsel the shaman and harpooner.

Ravens take many shapes and forms. Some ravens are key insiders and associates of your company, such as:

- An enthusiastic current client who introduces you to new prospects

- A member of your board of directors who brings a key prospect to your attention
- A friendly acquaintance of your company's leaders through affinity networks

Other ravens are your guides on the customer side, for example:

- A key member of your prospect's buying group who has brought you to the table
- An IT leader who wants to bring your service to his or her company
- An industry leader who recommends your services to others

Still another type of raven is a compensated intermediary, including

- A manufacturer's representative
- A contract salesperson

Regardless of their definition, all ravens are worthy of your time, attention, and nurturing, and should be engaged whenever you celebrate your whales.

Here's what you need to know about ravens.

- *Ravens are strong.* They are not afraid of temporary setbacks. Be sure that your ravens have the information, knowledge, and tools that they need to make your case.
- *Ravens are insightful.* They understand the internal politics of your whale. Seek their counsel about the interplay of events and resources in your customer organizations.

- *Ravens can navigate in the dark.* Whenever you're in the dark about what's going on with your whale, ask your ravens for help.

So how do you care for and feed your ravens? Three important concepts will help you to be successful.

First, ravens respect your recognition and appreciation of their role as relationship managers with your prospects and client. The more you acknowledge their role, the more time and energy they will devote to your interests. Celebrate the ravens!

Second, ravens reject any evidence that you are ignoring their advice or bypassing them in the political/decision-making processes. If you seek the advice of ravens, you need to follow it. Keep your raven at the table in each step forward with the prospect.

Finally, ravens believe in the concept of "giving forward." In many cases, your ravens bring you opportunities far beyond what you could reciprocate on a quid pro quo basis. They will be delighted if you acknowledge their wisdom, accept their gifts, and try to fulfill the role of the raven in your dealings with your employees, your prospects and clients, and your key business allies.

Lessons Learned

An early and important part of your internal celebration ought to be a peer review of lessons learned in this hunt. As soon as possible after you close the deal and launch the implementation phase, bring the boat and other key implementation players together for a structured, candid conversation about how well your teams performed and what will be the focus for improvement.

Please note we are not suggesting a top-down approach or a way to assign blame for any of the things that inevitably went wrong during the sales and services processes. Rather, we suggest a replicable process, conducted as a matter of routine, that is designed to help the village learn from experience, to reinforce the practices that consistently yield the best results, and to implement changes as a result of its learning.

Lessons Learned Principles

- *A routine, ordinary, friendly and low-risk process of assessment*
- *Undertaken by the people who were involved in doing the deal*
- *Focused on the company's whale-hunting model and maps*
- *A formal way of documenting that assessment*
- *A method of sharing lessons learned within the company, with the goal of improving the next hunt*

Search for Ambergris

We use the phrase "search for ambergris" to describe the process of growing sales within your existing accounts. And the ninth and final phase of the Whale Hunters' Process does indeed cycle back to the beginning, with the intent that your new contract with your new whale is only the first of many to come. Now is the time to begin thinking about your long-term relationships.

Ambergris is a rare substance produced only within the gut of a sperm whale. Used as a fixative for expensive perfumes and an aphrodisiac for kings, ambergris was for centuries considered to be more valuable than gold or precious gems.

The unknown areas of your whale will become the source of ambergris for your company. Perhaps you are dealing with one division of a company but not with others. Or you may have regional operations but not a national contract. Possibly you are selling one of your products or services but not others. Regardless of the current circumstance, unless properly managed, your knowledge and the whale's knowledge may inhibit additional business.

Your whale will come to believe that it knows you but may have your company slotted in a narrow space, or in a space you no longer wish to occupy, or in a space you have outgrown. Likewise, your village will come to believe that it knows the whale. But your villagers' whale knowledge may be limited to a particular buying group, division, or service area.

For these reasons, part of the celebration phase should include periodically holding a cross-functional meeting of people who "touch" this whale for the purpose of turning *common knowledge* (what you have learned individually) into *shared knowledge* (what your company can use to enhance the sales and delivery relationships).

As you do business with a whale, members of your team come to know the whale in different ways. Personal relationships, functional responsibilities, and historical contexts give you different perspectives. Unlike the dossier building and harpooner probing that characterizes the initial scouting activities, once the whale is your customer you have a great deal more firsthand knowledge at your disposal. But unless you have a plan and a process that capitalizes on that knowledge, you may remain in the time and place of the whale's initial contract with you.

So now is the time to begin a new series of companywide collaborative activities that will keep all of you attuned to new possibilities. We use an exercise called "See through the Fog" as a first step in this process. FOG stands for *fact, opinion,* and *gossip.*

Ask members of your cross-functional team who interact with the whale to make statements about the whale that will be relevant to your future business with the whale—particularly knowledge that would affect your ability to grow business with this whale dramatically in the next year. You gain industry knowledge by talking about your whale in a way that moves beyond current service or problem solving. Is there going to be a management change? Have they changed vendors on another product or service?

When you have a good list of statements, ask the team to debate whether each statement is fact, opinion, or gossip (FOG). For the factual statements, discuss how the shared knowledge may be relevant to your continued business with the whale. For statements marked as opinion, discuss the reasons for these opinions and how you might translate opinions into verifiable facts. Finally, attend to the gossip. Are there ways to track the gossip that will lead you to opinions and facts? Bottom line is this: What does your village know that individuals do not know?

Our client, Walker Information, specialists at customer strategies and loyalty, held a collaborative event to develop ambergris plans for several current whales. Table 11.1 gives an example of the whale knowledge they uncovered.

After completing this exercise, the team determined that four of the statements had the most relevance for additional business. These are marked with asterisks. Probably the single most important insight was about project coordination. Walker was concurrently managing a number of different projects for this whale. While each individual project was going well, Walker was not taking any specific internal steps to monitor whether the sum of these projects could yield any increased value to the whale. The whale saw them as a strong provider of services but was not yet envisioning them as

Table 11.1 See through the Fog

Statement	F Fact	O Opinion	G Gossip
**Our current position is the best it's been.	X		
They have requested a new proposal.	X		
**Projects are not effectively coordinated for maximum value.		X	
CEO is aware of us.	X		
Their initial interest is in our technology (how-to) not our advice.		X	
There are five competitors present.		X	
A new player is still forming perceptions of us.			X
Our operational quality is strong with them.		X	
**Our strategic value is not strong yet.		X	
They have decentralized buyers.	X		
They have internal conflicting factions—who are we aligned with?		X	
**We get conflicting directions from different factions.		X	
We have only 50% of the business opportunity that's available.		X	
They have referred us to other business.	X		
Our initial sponsor may be moving up within a few months.			X

a strategic ally. The collaborative activity, therefore, yielded significant insights into how to grow business with the whale. It provided specific guidance to the shaman, the harpooner, and the internal account managers on the focus of ongoing conversations with the whale.

Maintaining a continual collaboration around each whale will equip your village to grow more business rapidly and efficiently. The outcome of a FOG exercise should go back to your scouts, who can update the whale's dossier and include more information for tracking. The process of selling new business into an existing whale differs from selling to a new whale. In fact, in many cases, it is more complex because the whale has you pegged as a particular provider of a particular product or service. And since you are a most likely a smaller company than the whale, the whale may have a very narrow view of what you could in fact provide. As your business evolves, you increase your capabilities and your scope. Are you keeping the whale informed?

Another collaborative activity involves identifying features of your current business and relationship that may be assets or liabilities in your quest for future business with the whale.

- Your services (features, benefits, applications)
- Your competition (internal and external)
- Price, deliverables, terms, and conditions
- Your skill and reputation
- Customer contacts (needs, perceptions, relationships)
- Organizational culture and image (yours/theirs)
- Policies and procedures (yours/theirs)
- Decision process (complex versus simple, short versus long)

- Change (people, priorities, product or service)
- Timing, marketing conditions, economic climate

Once you have made a good list, determine whether these factors will be assets or liabilities. Then, while you are serving and celebrating the whale, your team can also attend to strategies that will strengthen your opportunities for more business with this whale.

For example, our client, WorkPlace Media, created a list of factors and strategies for one of their current whale clients. Table 11.2 lists only a few of the factors that their team identified.

Table 11.2 Whale Factors and Strategies

Factor	Strategies
Price	Predictive modeling Leverage the value of the channel
Change in our discount philosophy	Put it out in the open Ask many questions Incremental dollar discussion
Co-branding	Mock-ups Highlight convenience and awareness Leverage value of retailer's name Discuss shared budgets
Capitalize on recent success with a similar customer	White paper Case study Research analysis
We don't know who can make the buy for a national rather than regional account	Fact-finding conversation

Once you've identified relevant factors and outlined strategies to address those factors, you have the basis for a plan to prepare your company to grow business with this whale account.

Complete the Cycle

Celebrating the whale is a strategy that will keep your company focused on how to gain more business from your existing whale accounts. It will draw your customers closer to you, help them to differentiate you from your competitors, and attract their people to your people. As a consequence, the whale will extend you some patience, participate in teaching you how to do business with whales, and do more and bigger business with you over time.

The nine-phase Whale Hunters' Process doesn't end at phase nine. Rather, it allows you to recycle to phase one: know the whale. You are sending new information to the scouts, giving them better tracking tools. You are provisioning the harpooner to ask more and better questions, thereby increasing the village's information and continuing the process of translating isolated bits of information into knowledge and wisdom. You are preparing to launch a new boat for the same whale, perhaps focusing on a new division or a new region or introducing a new product or service.

So if you are a harpooner, a shaman, or a chief, imagine how your opportunities for business development and growth improve when your entire village continues to learn about the whale while delivering products and services to the whale. If you are a subject matter expert, imagine how much more new business and, therefore, revenue and resources, the harpooner can bring to your village with your help.

There is reason to celebrate! A whale will feed your village for a year. Celebrate your whales, and they will be reborn for new deals.

Celebrate the Whale Action Items

- *Conduct a lessons learned assessment to improve all processes for the future.*
- *Celebrate with the whale to communicate your gratitude.*
- *Feed your ravens to ensure new business.*
- *Search for ambergris and complete the cycle of service to every whale.*

Please visit www.thewhalehunters.com to download the sales process tools introduced in this chapter.

Epilogue

Let the Hunt Begin

WE ARE NOT MARINE BIOLOGISTS or anthropologists studying Inuit culture. We could not live more different lives. We advise the executive leadership team in fast-growth companies on how they can increase revenues and streamline their client list. Just like the Inuit, when your business reaches a certain stage of growth, you face a hard choice. You can make more and more small, safe sales, perhaps increasing the cost per sale, and certainly reducing the predictability of your sales and revenue cycle. Or you can concentrate on a smaller number of much bigger accounts, accounts that are harder to find, harder to land, and riskier to close and to deliver, but that will reduce your cost per sale, increase the predictability of your sales and revenue, and transform your company.

In these chapters, we have presented a system that will allow your fast-growth business to tolerate these risks, and we have encouraged you to implement this system, because the rewards of concentrating efforts on those big accounts outweigh the perceived safety offered by making many small sales. In business, as in the Arctic, it pays to become a whale hunter.

Consider your choices. Fewer than 1.5 percent of all companies in the United States ever grow above $25M in annual sales. That means that 98.5 percent of the companies never break through the glass ceiling of being a "small company." Business as usual—more of the same—will not allow you to make the rare transformation from "small company" to "big company."

We firmly believe that whale hunting offers a practical strategy for accelerated business growth. Our clients are living proof of this premise. The Whale Hunters' Process, customized to meet the unique criteria of your company's sales, can be replicated, improved, taught and learned, and taken to scale.

Whether your role is chief, shaman, harpooner, or subject matter expert, we invite you to introduce whale hunting into your village.

And we invite you to join The Whale Hunters community by logging into our website at www.thewhalehunters.com. All of the whale hunting tools introduced in this book are available for downloading from our Web site at no charge. You can sign up to receive our free biweekly newsletter, *Whale Hunters Wisdom*, which provides practical whale hunting advice, case studies, and comments from our clients. Discuss the ideas presented here in The Whale Hunters blog or in our online conversation space. Let us know what you have tried and how it is working. We look forward to meeting you online or in our travels as we talk with entrepreneurial sales- and businesspeople who are hungry for business growth.

Thank you for reading, and let the hunt begin!

Glossary

Ambergris—Rare and priceless substance produced deep within the gut of a sperm whale. The Whale Hunters use this term to represent additional value to be located within existing key accounts.

Boat—The team of villagers who hunt and capture a specific whale. The team includes a harpooner, shaman, and several oarsmen, subject matter experts (SMEs) who are needed to close a complex sale. SMEs on each boat represent all areas of the company. The village chief may also be involved.

Chief—President, CEO, founder, or other person identified as responsible for the company's growth and delivery of profits. This person is responsible for ensuring that the village is ready to harvest whales, recalibrates the target filter, and has final say as to whether or not a boat hunts.

Culture—The shared history that has made a company successful. As the village transforms into a whale hunting village, certain cultural beliefs change, but core values can be maintained and reinforced.

Harpooner—Salesperson who hunts whales. The harpooner is responsible for identifying the key decision makers inside a whale, qualifying the whale, generating interest in the whale, and bringing the whale through the sales process.

Harvesting—All activities that the boat and the village perform, from the point of agreement with a client through a defined period of time (usually the first 90 days of the contract).

Oarsmen—Key subject matter experts (SMEs) identified by the shamans and the village chief to participate in the sales process on the boat. These individuals have specific knowledge of elements of the products/services that the company is selling, and contribute to bringing the whale into the boat during the Whale Hunters' Process.

Process map—Visual and narrative representation of the series of choreographed activities in the village's whale hunting process. It includes every element of the nine-phase process—from knowing the whale to celebrating the whale—in the detailed series of steps defined for a particular village.

Scout—Marketing person who performs research on whales, generates prospect profiles on whales, monitors the market for "whale signs," and supports the harpooners per the shaman's direction.

Searching for ambergris (SFA)—A specific process and set of tools for capturing more business with the village's existing whale accounts.

Shaman—The direct supervisor of a group of harpooners. The shaman is responsible for training the members of the boat, facilitating the whale hunting process, communicating with the tribe, and managing the tracking process.

Subject matter expert (SME)—Villager with responsibilities in hunting and harvesting a specific whale. SMEs represent such areas as research and development, legal, human resources, information technology, operations, manufacturing, shipping, and others. They are selected as oarsmen when a particular boat is launched.

Target filter—Used as the evaluation chart for all prospective whales in the marketplace. Using the elements provided in the target filter, a score is given to each prospect whale, and that score determines whether and when the village hunts.

Village—All members of the company in all departments.

Whale—A sales prospect for a company that is whale hunting. The prospect is distinct from other sales prospects because it meets predefined criteria of size and desirability as a client.

Whale chart—Environmental scan of the marketplace and its inhabitants. This document identifies and qualifies the various opportunities in the marketplace by their desirable characteristics as a client.

Index

Page numbers followed by a *t* indicate tables.